"*Poetic Thinking. Now* is a passionate treatise, a courageous sketch of a new philosophical anthropology. The creative power of language is at its very heart. It is a critique of poetic reason and an engaging manifesto encouraging the reader to grasp the power of the poetic as a way to freedom. Now!"

Prof Dr Jürgen Trabant, *Professor Emeritus, Free University Berlin, Germany*

Poetic Thinking. Now

This book presents my concept of *poetic thinking* in the context of debates around the anthropological question, that is "what is being human?", building on "thinking language" and dialogical thinking, developing a *poetological anthropology*. It evokes political and social issues to demonstrate why poetics is of general relevance for our times. The chapters relate these questions to insights of quantum physics and neurosciences and discuss aspects of contemporary technology, media and medicine, employing notions such as *atmospheres, immanent transcendence, silence* and *presence* from contemporary thinkers. Poetic thinking considers the world in its togetherness, offering an alternative to the opposition of subject and object. It demonstrates the transformative power in the interaction of the form of language and the form of life. Poetic thinking takes place when a subject constitutes itself in creative and dialogical language, transforming its ways of feeling and thinking, in short, its way of perceiving the world.

Marko Pajević took up an EU funded Professorship of German Studies at the University of Tartu in January 2018 after holding positions at the Sorbonne, Paris IV and Queen's University Belfast, as well as Royal Holloway and Queen Mary University of London. He has published widely in German, English and French on poetics, with (co-)edited volumes on Paul Celan, multilingualism and the political, German and European poetics after the Holocaust and on the connection between poetry and musicality. He wrote monographs on Paul Celan and Franz Kafka. At the heart of his work stands the development of a poetological anthropology, as presented most prominently in a German-language monograph and in this book. His interest in *thinking language* resulted in special issues on Wilhelm von Humboldt and Henri Meschonnic and an English language Meschonnic Reader. Recently, he has worked on health and biopolitics with an edited volume and a forthcoming special issue, and on the notion of the abyss as a concept for cultural theory an edited volume is forthcoming. This is part of his overarching research project: see the website APT (Academia for Poetic Thinking): apt.ut.ee.

Routledge Focus on Literature

Literature, Education, and Society
Bridging the Gap
Charles F. Altieri

Shakespeare and the Theater of Pity
Shawn Smith

Trauma, Memory and Silence of the Irish Woman in Contemporary Literature
Wounds of the Body and the Soul
Edited by Madalina Armie and Verónica Membrive

Rilke's Hands
An Essay on Gentleness
Harold Schweizer

Orality, Form, and Lyric Unity
Poetics of Michael Donaghy and Don Paterson
Beverley Nadin

Milton and Music
Seth Herbst

Poetic Thinking. Now
Marko Pajević

For more information about this series, please visit: www.routledge.com/Routledge-Focus-on-Literature/book-series/RFLT

Poetic Thinking. Now

Marko Pajević

NEW YORK AND LONDON

First published in English 2024
by Routledge
605 Third Avenue, New York, NY 10158

and by Routledge
4 Park Square, Milton Park, Abingdon, Oxon, OX14 4RN

Routledge is an imprint of the Taylor & Francis Group, an informa business

© 2024 Marko Pajević

The right of Marko Pajević to be identified as author of this work has been asserted in accordance with sections 77 and 78 of the Copyright, Designs and Patents Act 1988.

All rights reserved. No part of this book may be reprinted or reproduced or utilised in any form or by any electronic, mechanical, or other means, now known or hereafter invented, including photocopying and recording, or in any information storage or retrieval system, without permission in writing from the publishers.

Published in German as *Poetisch denken. Jetzt* as part of the series Passagen Philosophie by Passagen Verlag 2022.

Trademark notice: Product or corporate names may be trademarks or registered trademarks, and are used only for identification and explanation without intent to infringe.

ISBN: 978-1-032-43521-3 (hbk)
ISBN: 978-1-032-43523-7 (pbk)
ISBN: 978-1-003-36770-3 (ebk)

DOI: 10.4324/9781003367703

Typeset in Times New Roman
by Newgen Publishing UK

Dedicated to the encounter

Contents

	Acknowledgements	*xii*
1	Poetic thinking. Now	1
2	Today's physical worldview	7
3	Neuroscience	14
4	The question of the human	20
5	Embodied thinking against body technologies	23
6	Life science and form of life	31
7	Attitude, mood, atmosphere	41
8	Immanent transcendence, silence and presence	45
9	Thinking language	51
10	Dialogical thinking	69
11	The meaning and purpose of poetic thinking	80
	Sources	*90*
	Index	*95*

Acknowledgements

Originally published as:
Poetisch denken. Jetzt, series Passagen Philosophie, Passagen Verlag, Vienna 2022. Translated from the German by Nicola Creighton.

I thank the University of Tartu for generously covering the translation costs.

1 Poetic thinking. Now

Crisis is non-stop, certainly. And in matters of the mind, that is just fine since crisis means turning-point, moment of decision, judgement. In many respects, one must of course be happy when everything is going smoothly and taking its course. In the world of the mind, however, smoothness means stagnation, and that would be the death of the mind. Thinking always means reconsidering, thinking beyond something, calling something into question. The mind must always begin anew, at every moment. It is the nourishing of the fire, living flame, not congealed form. Crisis therefore contains a moment of creativity, and thinking is itself a crisis phenomenon.

Today, however, there is an unmistakable feeling, nurtured by many interested parties, that we really are at a general turning point. It has become all too apparent that decisive changes are needed in our civilisation. We must begin in a fundamentally different way so that the crisis does not turn into a catastrophe. The problems range from environmental destruction to migration movements, from language regulation to the capitalist economy, from distributive justice and participation to the education system and the digitisation and virtualisation of the living environment, from familial to global togetherness – and all of this is exacerbated by the Covid-19 crisis and the war in Ukraine. These most recent shocks to our certainties throw all the older problems into even sharper relief. Trust in institutions and in the political system is on the wane. The increasing divisions in society, both economic and ideological, the digitally mangled public sphere with its manipulation, fake news and coarse culture of debate, and the struggle for the new instrument of power of our time, information, with the associated bio-politicisation of everyday life in a society of control, lead to cynical resignation.

Reform is needed everywhere, but the prevailing feeling is that things are being pushed farther and farther into the abyss. Especially when it comes to the ever more urgent issue of ecological transformation, we muddle along, mainly because the problems are so deeply rooted and everything is interconnected. Things are so closely intertwined and interdependent that there is nowhere to start unless we want to rip everything out all at once, which of course would not be possible.

The much-vaunted revolution must begin differently, on the one hand because we cannot wish for an actual bloody revolution, on the other because such a revolution would in the end only mean switching the crew, not the principles. True change occurs via the mind, as Kant recognised in his definition of Enlightenment. We must learn to think differently. Thoughts that change the world arrive on doves' feet, as Nietzsche put it. The thoughts are already there, the many must just be made aware of them so that they can take on social form. New ways of thinking must prevail to bring about profound, real change. In saying that, I am speaking also of the need for institutions that will ultimately have to anchor and spread such thought structures. But institutions can only ever be the result of what has been thought by many.

Incidentally, despite all the economic difficulties and worrying developments, in material terms, at least within our united Europe, things are still looking splendid. That may change again, but compared to earlier times, a poor person in Europe today, especially in northern and western Europe, is wallowing in luxury. Even if a European country were to experience complete economic collapse, the material impact would likely be very mild. There would certainly be social discord and turmoil, but hardly starvation. Elsewhere, things are undoubtedly different. The problems are there and should not be glossed over. Nonetheless, looking at the situation in western Europe, it cannot be denied: in terms of material advances, much has been achieved. This process will never be completed, of course, and for some time now, many social advances have been threatened by vested interests. In the face of this tendency, those advances must be defended and expanded. But in Europe also the poor often have the latest mobile phones and the biggest TVs, yet such consumption cannot make up for the lack. The main problem here – to which the other structural problems are related – is another: human life also needs a *why* for life, a purpose and a place in society. Without a purpose, every human order collapses. Our crisis is primarily a crisis of meaning. This is one of the reasons why the politics of identity, having developed from welcome emancipation efforts but then swung towards a destructive fragmentation of society, are so popular.

The feelings of lack, emptiness and frustration from which many people in the industrialised world suffer have causes other than material privation. Nevertheless, society in general seems to have lost awareness of what it is actually missing, because the majority of people are striving for more and more of what is materially available, only better, faster, louder, more colourful. It is an obvious trend that today the most conscious part of the population tends towards a reduction of things, looking for quality rather than quantity, while most are still and increasingly addicted to consumption: more meat, more sugar, more alcohol, more nicotine, more muscles, more extreme sports, more gadgets, more television, video clips, background music and noise pollution. None of this goes anywhere near the origin of the feeling of lack, however. The spiral just has to turn faster and faster so that people never stop and become aware of themselves.

It is not the outside, but the inside that is suffering a lack. In all of our material abundance, we are hungry for spiritual and meaningful things. Yet society is not aware of it. It is true that esoteric movements are extremely popular – a fact that illustrates the existing need for meaning – but we should not leave the discourse about the dimension of meaning in human life to so-called esotericism. We should try not to relinquish the achievements of the Enlightenment. Matters of the mind must be thought through; we must have solid foundations for our understanding of the world and of ourselves, and establish concepts that help us to accomplish that.

Nietzsche's Zarathustra speaks of the *great reason of the body*, which he contrasts with the small reason of the mind. In fact, the mind must be placed in the context of the greater reason of the body, in the sense that everything is rooted in living form and in the making of forms. The juxtaposition of mind and form is obsolete, a form without mind is nothing and a mind without form is unthinkable. In our materialism and our obsession with appearances and consumption – these days we obsessively consume even the appearances themselves – we have lost the category of spirit and can therefore no longer think about the problem at all. One-sided, economically oriented thinking has amputated the essential part of being human. Poetic thinking opposes this state of affairs. Spirit against money. Commerce cannot be a criterion for human life. Instead of taking in spiritual nourishment, we get filled, stuffed up, with material things or "entertainment". There is a system to it. And the suspicion arises that it suits parts of the elite just fine. "Sheeple" are needed that ask no questions – bread and circuses.

That keeps the masses calm – for the time being. But the undefined dissatisfaction is growing. It can be quelled but will resurface with ever more monstrous effects until eventually the monster runs amok altogether. Brexit has shaken the EU and, with it, the world order, and this danger is still at large. The growing political success of misogynist, xenophobic egomaniacs in recent years is a disturbing danger, also, in western democracies. And there are quite a few of his kind. Islamic State and religious fundamentalism in general, which likewise do not shy away from violence, are just the flipside of the problem, an overreaction to the need for meaning. Lacking stability in themselves, such collectives seek meaning through violence and must supply it from the outside, in the sense of differential belonging to a group or as an opponent. This is the typical mechanism of a weak ego bent on gaining an identity.

To create a real remedy for such meaninglessness, it takes more than consumption, it takes spiritual cultivation, but that has gone out of fashion. It is portrayed as strenuous. Fun and excitement are something else. There's the rub.

To begin with, we need a redefinition of pleasure. Instead of being "excited", i.e. being catapulted out of ourselves, we have to go within ourselves, confront ourselves with our inner being and work on ourselves. It must be made clear what enrichment and happiness we can reap from this, starting with the education system, then in working life and in leisure activities.

We need to understand that happiness requires self-sacrifice, that if things are to touch us, we first need to get involved. Only then can we be included in the context of life. So-called cheap thrills, which cost a lot of money these days, are only cheap in the sense that they demand nothing of us but money. We sit in front of them and are entertained, and our isolation remains intact. To be included in the world, we have to step towards it, we have to step into it, we have to get involved. Only then are we not alone, but connected.

I'm not panicking. The situation is urgent, but change is already in the air – it just needs to find forms to take hold. We live in turbulent times, times of crisis, in which decisions must be made that determine the future – decisions that determine whether there will be a human future. Or maybe just whether this future will be in harmony with what we like to call human today. What I call *poetic thinking* and what will be defined in more detail below will play a decisive role in this. And it is the elite who must risk this poetic thinking, because the danger is in those who lead, not those who follow. As things stand, we can only pin our hopes on outrage. Our leaders must be made to understand the need for a rethink.

Of course, poetic thinking can also be called something else, it's nothing new (what's new?), even if it has hardly ever appeared under this name and been applied to our situation in this way. At any rate, it is absent from the public way of dealing with the world. We need to include it in the ways we describe and thematise our life forms, because this is how we shape our ideas about our lives. In doing so, we also determine the goals that we pursue and the mechanisms that we use to shape human life in society. There have always been people who practised and cultivated this art of living. Terms with a similar import have been coined. One can call it care for the self, as Michel Foucault does, or ascesis, as Peter Sloterdijk calls it, or presence, new thinking, living thinking and so on. It is a greater kind of reason for the present. It has always existed and will always exist as long as there are humans because it is what we are and what is special about us. If it were to disappear, being human would lose its meaning.

If we are able to make our thinking poetic, we will emerge freer and happier from the turmoil of our time. If not, we shall perish one way or another. But since we always think poetically to a certain extent anyway, and actually cannot think any other way, I am sanguine about the future despite everything.

However – and the challenge remains indefinitely – we must allow this poetic thinking that is natural to us. We must nurture it for ourselves, and we must cultivate and develop institutions in which it can operate. Our society must give it a proper place where it can be effective, so that an appropriate worldview can be articulated and asserted. It must shape society and, to allow this to happen, we must be able to formulate consciously an idea of our own being on the basis of this kind of thinking.

So before humans can be ethical in the long run, we must first make them poetic, to paraphrase Schiller. We need a poetological anthropology as the basis for a new attitude towards our existence in this world. Only then can we meet the ecological, economic and technological challenges. And it must begin immediately and decisively, now.

This "now", however, also and essentially stands for the mode of the present. This presence – presence in a temporal and spatial sense – the here and now, being, is a central lever of poetic thinking. Poetic thinking offers the present a greater kind of reason. Everything boils down to presence, because everything begins from presence. But more on that later. After all, we must counteract *speed*, because dealing with speed, with the self-dissolving of Being in acceleration, is one of the main tasks that we are faced with today.

2 Today's physical worldview

To give my argument a solid basis, I should probably begin with scientific theses. That is something people like to see: it's all about measuring and proving and then you have an indisputable result, ideally with complex technology and display boards – brain scanners are always particularly impressive. After all, when so much money goes into research, the results must be significant, right? Technology is always a draw. Even in philology departments, expensive language labs are set up at the drop of a hat, while penny pinching hits literature seminars, which cost almost nothing anyway but could promote analytical skills and a real understanding of a culture.

The idea still prevails that the natural sciences are "hard" sciences, while the humanities offer only speculation, if not mere enthusiasm and fancy. In the dominant world language, English, the latter are not even accorded the status of science. The "Geisteswissenschaften" (the German means sciences of the mind or spirit) are simply the *humanities*, that are somehow considered a useless luxury and are accordingly being diligently curtailed at universities. And why as a native speaker of English one should learn another language at all is something many a university chancellor or educational policymaker has great trouble grasping – after all, the world is learning English, so learning any foreign language is simply a waste of time.

Funnily enough, science has been proving the opposite for a whole century. Today's world with its nuclear physics, its chemistry, its electronics and all of its information technology is based on long-recognised physical principles that prove that matter is not so hard and unassailable, and, what's more, that it is not even made up of matter – gasp! – but rather of something that comes much closer to the spiritual.

The classic physical worldview assumes that everything is composed of the smallest, indivisible atoms. These particles are permanent, they are matter that endures over time and provides physical continuity. This is the basis of so-called reality, which consists of things (Latin: res). Changes are brought about by rearrangements of these fundamental particles. On this conception, matter clearly comes first, whereas forms and shapes are composed of matter, that is, they come second. Forms change over time, as a result of changing constellations of constant matter.

Our thinking is still having a hard time detaching itself from these ideas even though modern physics exposed them as wrong more than a century ago. Today's physics is based on a different model that has long formed the basis of our social functioning. In 1900, Planck observed light waves behaving like particles. Einstein's theory of relativity followed in 1905. Rutherford discovered elementary particles in 1911. Close on their heels came Bohr's notion in 1913 of the "smearing" of electrons. 1923 brought de Broglie's interpretation of immaterial vibration, with Heisenberg's uncertainty principle following in 1927. This entire physical revolution is still hardly anchored in general thought. And this despite the fact that these findings have proven to be extremely efficient in "reality".

It is obviously so much easier to deal with fixed thingliness than with a processual notion of reality. But the material world is only appearance. There is no material reality independent of the viewer. Objectivity and subjectivity are inseparable; actuality has a holistic structure. The so-called realists live in an illusion. There is a difference between reality as composed of the "res", the things, and actuality as determined by the totality of all effects. However, non-things such as attitudes and atmospheres also have an effect. But more on that later – at any rate, actuality is more comprehensive than reality. (The German terms "Wirklichkeit" for "actuality" and "Realität" for "reality", are often used as synonyms but the former comes from "wirken", that is, to act, to have an effect.)

Modern physics broke matter down even further, and it turned out that atoms are far from being the smallest indivisible particles. Rather, they, in their turn, consist of so-called elementary particles, which actually represent more of a constellation, an oscillation, from which the smallest particles of matter are then composed. Indeed, with further research, it turns out that nothing material is left at all, but that everything only emerges from form, i.e. from a relationship. Matter is therefore not composed of particles of matter at all, but relationships. In other words, something immaterial, more like vibrations, is at the origin of reality. It is physics itself that has proven that matter comes second, and ephemeral form and relationship first.

So we must think of matter in a completely different way. Matter is just a hardened relationship structure, a form that has become lifeless. Reality is the slag of the process of actualisation, a residue, that which has separated itself from life. In actuality, the origin of all matter is the life process itself. In actuality, there is no solid reality, but an open and constantly flowing process of creation, a constant arising and passing away. Figures are formed anew at every moment. There is no actual continuity of matter.

Of course, most things take form pretty much as they were before, and in the case of things in general one shouldn't expect too much imagination. The famous philosophical table usually remains a table in the next moment, quite simply because it is not blessed with an exceptional imagination. The more spiritually alive something is, the greater the change. In general, however, quantum physics has made it clear that things are processes. Electrons do not travel in orbits from one place to another, rather they dissipate in one place and regroup elsewhere. Beam me up, Scotty!

It is of course a matter of perspective. At what level are things being observed? For reasons of practicality, hardened reality is taken more seriously than its origin, that which is spiritually alive. It is also apparent that it has proven itself. This probation, on the other hand, must be updated at any moment if it is to remain alive. Probation must be proof in the sense of truth. The thing only preserves its validity if it proves itself again and again in life at every moment. What is exists as such only as a process.

From all this it follows that our scientific-analytical approach to the world can convey a great deal of knowledge but does not do it justice in every regard. Properly considered, the separation into components is an outdated view. We can also safely shelve the project of completely explaining the world. There are fundamental limits to knowledge. We will never know everything because the world simply can't be fully defined – it's constantly changing. Any individual part is always just part of the whole. The entire world is one entity in which everything is in constant flux. So if we want to get closer to reality, we have to view it as a whole and as a unit. Everything is connected.

That of course does not necessarily lead to greater accuracy. Science strives for the clearest possible statements. So it has to abstract from this great spiritual context of the world, ultimately having to simplify in completely inadmissible ways. That is of course fundamentally necessary: our linguistic conditionality already forces us to use linear representations, since we must put one word after the other, although what is represented in such a linear manner corresponds more to tangles than unrolled ribbons. But that's not a problem, it's our way of rubbing against actuality and getting involved in it. The world is always just the world for humans, and we have to construct it for ourselves, each one of us. And that keeps us very busy. At every moment we are working on this world of ours in connection with everyone else. Everyone lives in their own world, but mine is the right one – everyone can claim that about themselves because it *is* their own world. We should just always make sure to bear in mind that we are getting along by means of makeshift constructions – nothing more solid or abiding than that – in creating and formulating our consciousness of the world.

We all know that when we truly immerse ourselves in actuality, we are not capable of clear awareness. In such moments, we are usually speechless and otherwise not quite there with ourselves but simply part of the world, absorbed in the big picture, the oceanic feeling. According to quantum physics, every clear notion is a wrong notion, reality is rather blurred by dint of our faculties. We need clear, i.e. fragmentary, analytical thinking in order to find our way around and deal with the world. However, we also need holistic thinking in order to reflect on what in fact constitutes actuality.

However, if everything is created anew at every moment, then everything is in fact always possible. Maybe not quite everything, but plenty. Reality has the quality of potentiality, it can be this but it can also be that, we will see. This potentiality keeps the future open, that's why there is a future. Without it, the future would be an absurd concept. We don't know it and we will never know it, it is coming towards us: avenir, Zukunft, as the French and German terms indicate, meaning that which is "to come" and "coming towards" us. It is yet to reach us, all the time. But actuality is potentiality and we are part of it. That's why we can always shape it. The potentiality is within us and we ourselves are potentiality.

This potentiality arises from relationality – ours and that of the world. That's why we can't know it, we can only live it. Any analytical understanding goes against the nature of it and requires, so to speak, a change into another mode of being. That is why we have knowledge that relates to individual things, but that does not reach the dimension of meaning. The dimension of meaning goes beyond conceptual thinking. So we can and should make an effort to understand the world, but in doing so we will always come up against limits that in principle cannot be overcome, because the world cannot be understood. Rather, there can be a momentary unity in which the world opens up and one merges into it – receives it and enters it. What is important here is not the subject that experiences, but the relationship in which it finds itself.

One of the main reasons why we perceive the world today as so terribly complex is our desire to take it apart and control it. It has always been unmanageably complex but has only become so unbearable on account of our scientifically hewn worldview. If we accept that we don't necessarily have to dissect the world, its complexity is no longer so oppressive. The problem belongs to our western society in the wake of the Enlightenment. Goethe has his Mephistopheles mockingly describe the analytical approach:

> He who would study organic existence,
> First drives out the soul with rigid persistence;
> Then the parts in his hand he may hold and class,
> But the spiritual link is lost, alas!
> (Translation Bayard Taylor)

Other cultures, which definitely represent the majority of humanity, have completely different ideas and are not familiar with these problems. We tend to reduce everything to what is objectively identifiable and to dismiss everything else as flights of fancy, figments of our imagination that cannot be taken seriously.

But what is really important in life is precisely what cannot be measured objectively. Perhaps at this point it should be recalled that even in today's western society, our being and our attitude towards life depend less on material things and more on relationship structures. Every experience is the result of a relationship between the experiencer and the experienced. In human life, everything still revolves primarily around the need for love, recognition and security, i.e. for connectedness and connection. Certainly, material things are involved, but it cannot be reduced to the material. The moment a subject defines objects from this primary relationship, an abstraction takes place that establishes "objectivity" and erases the particular relationship at hand. In this way, the lived actuality becomes a manageable reality.

Physics has meanwhile progressed so far that it hardly ever operates with physically perceptible phenomena. It is still taking measurements, except that it must realise that the results cannot be understood with our possibilities of perception. It must therefore produce models that convert a reality that does not correspond to our concepts into a coherent whole. String theory leads to ideas of various other dimensions that we cannot understand; parallel worlds are assumed to justify the measurement results. To reiterate, we are not talking about science fiction here, nor about esoteric extremists, but about "hard" science, natural scientists, top researchers at the best universities in the world.

As early as the 1950s, Werner Heisenberg had established that quantum physics can only be described in parables: our linguistic logic lacks the concepts to grasp this model. It is interesting that this physicist and philosopher drew attention to the fact that poetic speech offers and houses ways of perceiving the world that linear-rational speech cannot, and above all that such a specifically poetic representation of the world does more justice to the actuality of the circumstances. It is time to draw the conclusions from these insights and to restore to poetic thinking a more important place in our social order.

Perhaps the moment has come to hint at one aspect of the poetic: its holistic nature. I will take the poem as an example, but of course that's just the conventional form. The division into prose and poetry has nothing to do with the poetic; the poetic as such of course also exists elsewhere, outside of the literary. My definition is: *the poetic is what cannot be said otherwise*, or, extended to the extra-linguistic – *what is itself only in precisely this form.*

So a poem only makes sense as an organic whole, we cannot take it apart and break it down into its component parts and then expect to find the meaning of the poem in those individual parts. If we wanted to proceed in that way and, like a proper analyst, wanted to put those elements in a clear order, list the words alphabetically or even group all the letters, then we would have cooked its goose. Unfortunately, this is exactly what happens in so many processes of our high technology. All genetic manipulation operates in exactly this way. An element is added to or taken from a coherent whole, which has usually developed over thousands of years as a coordinated ensemble, and it is then assumed that the whole is the same, only better. The fact that this intervention destabilises the entire structure and leaves nothing as it was before is considered worthy only of disregard.

That can work out fine. A poem does not necessarily deteriorate when a word is exchanged. It just becomes different, not only where there is a different word, but everywhere, since the poem is the form as a whole and not a collection of elements. It's more than the sum of its parts. Its meaning is also not the added meaning of the individual elements. Yet even literary studies find it very difficult to talk about the poem as a whole and usually approach the phenomenon in this destructive way. We must develop forms for poetic thinking that do justice to the context of life. While it may be a paradoxical undertaking to want to speak conceptually about that which eludes concepts, it is just here that the challenge begins: our ways of speaking and our concepts need more work.

3 Neuroscience

If I want to say something about thinking, I can't afford to exclude brain research. After all, it has now become the leading science. The problem with brain research is, of course, that it so often confronts us with an astoundingly truncated structure of argumentation, which goes something like this: when a person feels love and we can identify activity in certain areas of the brain, then we know what love is: a reflex caused by chemical processes. Or: if I can activate certain areas of the brain with electronic currents, giving many test subjects a feeling of revelation, then we have established what religion is, namely a stimulation of these parts of the brain. As early as the eighteenth century, people were very busy trying to locate the seat of the soul. It was concluded that it was behind one of our ears.

I must admit that it is a mystery to me how such answers can even remotely satisfy anyone, let alone such highly intelligent people as neuroscientists, highly educated researchers. All that these methods prove is that there are correspondences between body and mind. Foot reflexology also works, but that doesn't mean that my stomach upset is actually in the sole of my foot, let alone was caused by it.

Now, neurobiologists are of course anything but stupid and very few will have genuinely imagined that they had really revealed the secret of life and feelings with such measurements, even if for a time they might have entertained such hopes. By now, however, brain research has fortunately left such simplistic unilaterally biological explanations behind. Having concentrated for a long time on collecting and documenting scientific facts and thinking in a materially determined way, neuroscientists have evidently recognised for some time now that humans cannot be reduced to their brain: this is merely a part of the human being. Reason is greater. The natural sciences are opening up to the realisation that "human nature" is also essentially shaped by culture. Neurobiologists now readily acknowledge that social contexts and emotional, pre-rational relationships have a profound impact not only on our behaviour but also on our biological makeup.

So genes do not decide everything, and we are not determined by them. Rather, they are a relatively open system that not only sends out signals, but also reacts to signals and is formed in that context. Our brain, then, works the way we have trained it to work – it is the result of our behaviour and is therefore not fixed, but changeable. We can constantly shape our brain and how it works – it is ultimately less biologically and more socially determined. Likewise, we now hear from evolutionary anthropologists that genetics are simply not sufficient to explain the most important cognitive achievements of humankind: the development time has been far too short for that. It was cumulative cultural development that gave rise to the vast difference between humans and other primates. The crucial inexplicable leap in this development is the recognition of one's own kind as intentional spiritual beings, beings like oneself. This particular form of social understanding then produces particular forms of cultural inheritance that accumulate over time, with each individual human child absorbing what their culture offers them and developing their very own understanding from it.

The reason for humanity's success on earth lies precisely in the extraordinary flexibility of the brain. Rather than being strongly determined, neural pathways only develop in the course of life and should then remain as changeable as possible. This particular human quality probably came to be expressed due to a lack of real physical strength. Humans can do everything a little and nothing outstandingly. The specialists in the animal kingdom were able to conquer their niche, in which they then established themselves, on account of their speed, their strength, their ability to fly, their ability to see. Humans, for their part, are not competitive in all those specialisations, so they had to assert themselves differently, namely through their extraordinary versatility and adaptability. The more flexible the interconnections in the brain are, the easier it is to bring together the wide variety of perceptions that humans have. The human brain is therefore relatively unpredetermined by genetics, but rather an open construction that can change over and over. Depending on the requirements of the life situation, it restructures itself repeatedly. This enables quick reactions and effective adaptation to new living conditions.

It is possible, then, to develop and stabilise neural connections that were not yet fixed at birth in different ways and according to circumstance. People's individual perceptions and experiences become anchored in neural wiring patterns only over the course of their lives. Such experiences and structures made in their respective living conditions can then also be passed on to subsequent generations, which brings us to cultural evolution.

Once a species has occupied and secured a niche, the latter can be maintained by fairly primitive brain structures. Efficiency is achieved through instinctive security, in other words quick reaction and unscrupulousness. However, the greater the complexity and the more changeable the living conditions, the more complex the brain structures required. For a sense of community, which is of vital importance for survival in such difficult living conditions, the ability to relate, to consider others and to maintain a sense of belonging are important skills. In humans, such factors are considered when choosing a partner, in the sense of Darwinian survival of the fittest. The fittest is not necessarily the fittest physically but rather the most suitable. Such social skills, and with them the undefined brain structures and neurological pathways required for them, can spread and assert themselves in complex living conditions. Unscrupulous strength is not the most suitable quality when it comes to the good of the community.

Of course, the conditions are by no means the same for everyone. If I grow up in circumstances that, for existential reasons, only allow for certain behavioural patterns, or if I am traumatised due to my social environment and the unfavourable behaviour of those I care about, I will be forced to develop one-sided, entrenched brain and behaviour patterns with which to react to such situations. Such patterns can work very successfully in certain situations, but in others they will lack the necessary flexibility and fail miserably.

Accordingly, flexible neural wiring patterns are desirable for a socially functional, adaptable society, while one-sided, deadlocked pathways are better avoided.

We humans have the chance, then, to programme our brains ourselves by the way we use them. This opportunity needs to be maintained. How do we do that? By being mindful of our own environment. Feeling involved and affected by the world is the best precondition for challenging old ways and redesigning our programming. Any defence against being affected prevents the most comprehensive use of the brain. So, to carry forward the recipe for human success, we need to use our brains as fully as possible. We must not be too fixed, nor pursue anything specific from the outset, developing rather as many different modes of perception as possible and remaining open to the unexpected. That may also be the meaning of Goethe's famous poem:

> I was walking
> In the wood alone,
> And intended
> To look for nothing.
> In the shade I saw
> A little flower growing
> Gleaming like stars,
> Lovely as eyes.
> I was going to pick it,
> When gently it said:
> Must I be picked
> To wilt and die?
> I dug it out
> With all its roots.
> Took it to the garden
> Of my pretty home.
> And planted it again
> In a quiet corner;
> Where still it grows
> And continues to bloom.
> (Translation
> Richard Wigmore)

Here, too, we are dealing with mindfulness, attention and holism. Empathising with the flower, looking at it holistically and finding a compromise solution is a clear win-win here.

This shift in the neurosciences can be traced back to the "discovery" of so-called mirror neurons in 1995. It is questionable whether it makes sense to speak of discovery with something so obvious, but it meant the phenomenon was now also experimentally, i.e. empirically scientifically, proven and named and that is a good thing. Mirror neurons are nerve cells that implement a specific programme in their own body, triggered by simply experiencing – for example through observation, but also through verbal mediation – a behaviour implemented by others. So if someone smiles at you, you smile back, if they yawn, you yawn too, and if they cross their legs, you do the same. These are *resonance phenomena*: you tune into the wavelength of the other person and are therefore in harmony. Body postures are mirrored, but also moods and feelings. That is the basis of *sympathy*, as the Greek meaning of the word says: to suffer with another. If someone shows me that they understand my feelings and moods and goes along with them, then I like them – expressionless people have a harder time on that front. So it's all about empathy: socially connecting ideas are activated and felt in the recipient's brain and then find their external expression when mirrored.

Everyone is born with a suite of mirror neurons, but as we have already seen, their fate is in our hands, our own and those of the environment. Mirror neurons must be activated and used. If they are not nurtured, they wither away. If we don't stimulate and develop these mechanisms through use, we won't have them at our disposal. It's a subtle system. Use it or lose it.

All this makes it clear that we need a partner to develop them. Humans need stimulation from others, in fact it is necessary for survival. In the thirteenth century, the Staufer Emperor Frederick II ran an experiment to discover the original language. He had children nursed by wet nurses, but the wet nurses were not allowed to communicate with the children, the idea being that they, the children, would speak of their own accord and so learn the "natural" language of humanity. The children of course did not speak, they wasted away and died.

Man cannot live without being spoken to. The fact that this also applies to adults can be proven using the example of voodoo: if a community sentences a member to death, the condemned person actually dies within a short time, without external influence and completely inexplicably in biological terms, simply by complete exclusion from the community. This would be difficult to replicate in today's western societies, but it still worked in Central and South America in the twentieth century.

It is not only actions but also language that can cause the mirror neurons to fire. Through language we can evoke reflections of our ideas in the other person and create mutual understanding. That is why language acts are just such: acts. They can be felt physically, as a slap or as a caress.

The important lesson to be gleaned here is that everything that is perceived and spoken leaves its mark on us. Our gestures and actions are not ineffective, our words are not smoke and mirrors. Neither are the images, sounds and words we are exposed to. So we don't just feed on food and drink, but on the whole world.

We should bear this in mind when we fill our channels of perception with all sorts of unpleasantries. Nowadays, media and hectic city life overwhelm us with stimuli that we must either mirror or fend off. Nietzsche said that one should surround oneself with perfect things because they teach hope. He's right, nurturing the beautiful and harmonious, cultivating it in our own lives, is a formative factor of being. So, instead of always just paying attention to our diet in relation to food, we should also cultivate a *dietary awareness of the mind* and serve it up only selected things.

Today's neuroscience confirms that behaviour also changes our biological, genetic being. The environment we surround ourselves with also shapes our neurobiological structures. We are communal beings; our programmes of action and feeling are not purely individual but also determined by resonance.

Flexible patterns of behaviour and perception, wholeness, resonance and cultivation: these are the terms that we must retain for poetic thinking from this foray into the natural sciences.

4 The question of the human

We are already on the subject the entire time, because poetic thinking inscribes itself in the anthropological question: *What does it mean to be human?* And that is the basic question that has also guided our reflections on physics and neuroscience and that is generally in the background of all human activities. Asking this question is actually an essential part of being human, it is an expression of our particularity: self-reflection. Accordingly, we always have an image of the human, even if we are not always aware of it.

The new potential of intervening biologically in humanity offered by genetic engineering, coupled with new findings in brain research and the formative influence of new media, has led to a destabilisation of our image of humanity. It has as a result been changing for some time now, with new visions of being human undergoing intensive development. Such visions are by no means meaningless mental games of head-in-the-clouds philosophers; on the contrary, they are highly relevant to action. Depending on the image humans have of themselves, they will act in one way or another. A person who sees him- or herself as a creature of God is likely to behave differently from someone who sees him- or herself as an ape that has made it or as a flawed machine. It is also very important whether you want to surrender to your nature and instincts or define yourself as an ethical and moral being who wants to overcome your weaker self and educate yourself towards higher things. Such self-images guide energies and decisions and have very concrete practical effects.

What is certain, at any rate, is that as humans we are not only given natural talents, but we can shape ourselves. Otherwise, culture really wouldn't matter. And for this formation the idea of oneself gives the direction. Right now, at a time when our society has to make a range of decisions on legislation especially in the medical field, the image of humanity is decisive.

Poetic thinking sees itself as a contributor to these important current shifts; it would like to design a poetological anthropology, that is, to promote an image of the human in which the poetic, in a sense that has yet to be specified, is afforded an appropriate space in the setting of aims for our life forms and ideals. The cultivation of such an image of the human, which allows both a sustainable togetherness of all people with each other, but also of people with animals and nature, is absolutely essential for our survival given the tasks we are faced with today.

The pragmatic anthropology that goes back to Immanuel Kant is the programme of constant work on oneself: human beings are destined to cultivate and civilise themselves and to develop their morality, as opposed to indulging their natural inclination to lazy living. This bourgeois project of enlightenment contains great potential for emancipation; every single person has the opportunity to climb to the highest heights and to develop their individuality and their subjectivity as much as possible. By making ourselves our life project, we can rise above the initial circumstances of our life. Unfortunately, however, such an idea also contains the potential for totalitarianism. For every single human being, the process of enlightenment is a terrible machine of repression: we are no longer allowed to pursue our base desires and must cope with quite an amount of frustration. But beyond that, in the name of an ideal, all other ideals can also be quashed. Above all, however, while reason was being produced, unreason also came about, namely through the repression of the *other of reason*. Nature, the body, imagination, desire, feelings and the unconscious must be warded off, excluded and repressed so that the rational subject can rule. This naturally leads to an unhappy consciousness and a limitation of human possibilities.

Obviously, I'm not advocating living out one's human instincts with abandon, that would mean all manner of murder and manslaughter and rape, but an awareness of the limitations of "reason" and an inclusion of the other in human self-understanding is not only closer to reality and healthier, but also more socially cohesive in a global world in which we must understand other ways of life.

A single, normative anthropology is apparently no longer conceivable nowadays; a universally valid definition of the human is impossible and no longer even desirable. The talk of "subhumans" that can be derived from such discourses has caused too much harm. Incidentally, philosophical anthropology, beginning with Kant, never really tried to provide such an overarching framework, but always pointed out the historical and cultural character of the human. Yet if humans are conditioned by the circumstances of their lives, they are perforce not the same everywhere and at all times. They are a product of various factors. It is precisely this fact that lends such weight to the processes of human self-creation. Poetic thinking wants to think these processes. The word *poetic* comes from making or producing. Poetic thinking, then, thinks how, as humans, we create ourselves.

5 Embodied thinking against body technologies

Today there are strong indications that people are no longer working on themselves but allowing themselves instead to be made by means of various interventions from outside, using technology. I would like to briefly present these tendencies in the following in order to signal the dangers involved and to clarify why poetic thinking is so necessary today.

The plethora of new options for intervening in the body together with the ideal physique promoted by the media produce an increasingly technical conception of the body. The scientific worldview that emerged from the Enlightenment already considered the human body analytically, i.e. it disassembled it into its component parts and regarded it as an object. The associated division into mind and body transformed embodied thinking into thinking about the body. We must distinguish between *the body we have* and *the body we are*. We are a part of nature – that will have dawned on us at the latest with our grasp of the environmental problem – and are nature ourselves. We have to keep becoming aware of our body during daily life in order to integrate into the world in this way. A conscious handling of food, physical exercise and bodily love are examples of such bodily thinking, in which human beings identify with their body.

Of course, for certain cognitive processes it is useful to consider the human body as an object. But such an attitude leads to problems for our self-understanding as human beings. We then no longer see the unity of mind and body, but can view our physical development as independent of our inner being. This has an impact on our definition of human beauty and on our self-image.

After all, today with the help of plastic surgery you can more or less buy a body – not the body of another but your own! But then you are not really that body, you rather own it as an object.

As early as 1890, Oscar Wilde described in his allegory *The Picture of Dorian Gray* what can happen when the unity of body and mind is broken. Enchanted by his own beauty captured in a portrait, Dorian Gray makes a pact with the devil: he sells his soul to retain his youthful beauty, allowing the effigy to age instead of him. Freed from the consequences of his actions for his appearance, he becomes increasingly ruthless, while his innocent mien allows him to deceive those around him all the better. After many years of nefarious living, he looks at the hidden portrait and, horrified by the ugly grimace that looks back at him, reflecting his interior self, he ends his life. This extraordinarily moral story by the aestheticist Wilde illustrates his aphorism that from the age of thirty we are responsible for our own appearance. For we are a body, and the body that we have is not independent of our spirit. It is the spirit that builds the body for itself, as Schiller put it. And that's good. If we were able to control and shape our bodies so independently of our minds, we would run the risk, according to Wilde, of the ethical brutalisation of Dorian Gray and an inhuman society.

Well, these days with plastic surgery and liposuction such fantasies seem within reach. For those who possess the necessary funds, the industry promises a fountain of youth. They are promises – if you look closely at the faces that have been lifted and manipulated in this way, you are more likely to see the distorted image than the youthful Dorian Gray. Likewise, all those oomphed-up breasts are no doubt more for viewing from afar than for direct contact. But that's consistent: it's not really about human contact with these self-editings, it's about image. You want to be a *star*, far away in the sky: look at me, but don't get too close!

At any rate, people's self-image must be quite damaged if they believe that youth and beauty can be achieved through purely external manipulation. The feeling for the connection between body and mind has apparently been lost, the holistic human being is out of joint and its desires are not in harmony with being. No longer part of the world with their being, today's humans want to consume the world as much as possible. The world is an object, so is the body, including one's own. So it can also be manipulated, since in this perspective it is outside us. Plastic surgery, and even more so genetic engineering, allows us to see the body as an artefact. It is material that is worked on – independently of the spirit.

It is no longer about *humanitas*, that is, being humane, but about *hominitas*, being a human. We are dealing here with hominal technologies that, with their possibilities of enhancement, propagate an ideal human body. As such, this is an old programme. Working on yourself to make the best of yourself is an honourable undertaking. However, it depends very much on how it is done.

Let's look at this in the media and in medicine. It is obvious that the media propagate an ideal body. However, they no longer only do this through the role model function that publicly displayed bodies assume. Certainly, it's the showbiz stars who embody, if they don't outright create, such ideals, but even their images are digitally manipulated as a matter of course, adjusted and enhanced in the virtual photo lab to match the ultimate ideal.

Looking at the networking forums in the media, it becomes apparent that these have to a large extent become body-swapping exchanges. Physical merits are touted and aligned with market trends. It is a commodities market in which the body has a market value which can be increased through investment – surgical interventions or bodybuilding – to get a better deal. Bodybuilding still requires your own willpower and effort, but in contrast to sports (turning a blind eye to doping for a moment), bolstered by protein supplements. Cosmetic surgery, however, is a wave of the fairy wand once the money has changed hands.

Television content such as surgery shows are extreme examples of how the ideal body is promoted. Their existence as well as that of internet platforms, for example YouTube and other websites, especially YouPorn, is testimony to the pervasive need to market one's own body. It is primarily about turning a top profit, but not many reach that level so they have to content themselves with the ego-boost they can get from their physique.

Sexuality as portrayed on the internet is at any rate the best example of this problematic body image. The insane proliferation of pornography via this medium promotes a machinic understanding of man. Allegedly one in six Germans has made at least one porn video. In porn, there is often quite frank discussion of the human as a "fucking machine", and people are also portrayed as such. Sexuality is thus conveyed as a mechanical activity – detached from any erotic approach in which physical attraction goes hand in hand with a spiritual connection.

But things are not so different in medicine either. Of course, there is a very tangible financial interest at play there. The pharmaceutical industry has good reason to promote the notion that taking enhancers creates hope for the future, not just of being pain-free, but also of delivering better performance. Without wanting to delve into side effects, we should ask ourselves whose interest this boosted performance is serving. Is it about competitive advantage? But if these resources were available to all, it would be a level playing field. Or will the gap between the poor beggars who can't afford enhancers and the wealthy ones who can just widen and society drift farther and farther apart?

Despite a growing awareness of the importance of holistic healing approaches, institutions still function largely on the principle of healing by means of external products. Maybe it is simply a matter of staff shortages – medicines seem to be cheaper than human attention, or rather, influential lobbies make a lot of money from the former, while the latter generally has less traction. Even in psychiatry, people are mostly treated as corporeal beings. Psychiatrists really should know better, yet here too the self-definition of the role no longer requires the claim of lasting healing, but merely that of symptom suppression. If this results in a lifelong intake of psychotropic drugs for the patient, then the industry thrives and with it the system.

It is easy to see how the human being as a subject is given short shrift here and treated rather as an object of external manipulation. Instead of understanding the human as a unity of mind and body, it is reduced to biochemical processes in the body. With all the successes of this system, we must be clear that it works according to industrial criteria. The doctor has become a technician and salesperson, the patient a customer, and the hospital an industrial company. The medicine is to restore the body machine, it is part of the commodity operation. Man has thus also become a commodity. In this logic he has become a machine man. If a part stops working, it will be replaced or repaired. Incidentally, a French doctor, the radical materialist and enlightener Julien Offray de la Mettrie, wrote a book in the middle of the eighteenth century, in which he spoke precisely of this machine man, *L'homme machine*.

At that time, this certainly included the potential for liberation from oppressive structures, but today the situation has changed and reducing people to their bodies has itself become a mechanism of manipulation and ultimately repression.

It makes a crucial difference whether a person improves his body through his own effort, or whether this happens through external manipulation. In the first case, he acts as a physical-spiritual entity that uses discipline and willpower to develop towards an ability or quality. In the second case, the mind doesn't matter, the human being is just an objectified body that has been invested in with the aim of functioning smoothly or more successfully in economic terms and with reliable labour output as the main objective.

The hominal-technological image of man equipped with a body that is ideal in machine terms has of course significant social effects. It weakens the self-esteem of real people who unsuccessfully emulate this virtual ideal. It weakens the bonds of couples who are constantly being compared to their own market value and asked if they can't find a better deal. In times of internet dating, when you can try out a new partner every day in metropolitan areas, there is potentially always someone better – which makes a real relationship more challenging. It weakens reality, one lives in an ever-deferred potentiality.

Above all, of course, the implications of violence are divested of reality when the idealised human body, completely detached from any emotional-affective workings, appears and acts in video games and, despite all the grotesque depictions of violence, takes on a role model function. In summary, one can say that the hominal-technological image of man is not about the education of a subject, but about the change and optimisation of an object. This also weakens education. In this new perspective, humans should no longer be perfected through education and culture, as the humanistic tradition of enlightenment advocated, but instead physiologically and genetically. If Nietzsche's superman was still all about surpassing himself intellectually, through noble thinking and acting and disciplined work on himself, then the goals and methods of today's self-optimisers correspond much more to those of the "last humans" despised by Nietzsche, who strive only for comfort and an easy life. And these goals are presented as so easily attainable, via external manipulation, you don't even have to make an effort or give up anything – *you can have it all. Just sign here...*

If you want to resist these promises, you have to have something to oppose them with, something you simply cannot achieve on this external path, but for which you have to take the arduous path of inner commitment. You have to know what you're missing if you think you'll find happiness by external means. We need knowledge of a better alternative, embodied thinking instead of corporeal thinking.

All of this may sound like an exaggeration. Of course it's nice when medicine can relieve the pain – no question about that. But the transitions are fluid and more and more mechanisms creep in, in very small steps, so that we will hardly notice it when one day we have completely internalised body thinking. Incidentally, some radical representatives of machine thinking hold very influential positions. They peddle contemporary versions of the myth of immortality or fantasies of omnipotence in which man wants to assume the role of God. These self-proclaimed visionaries and human creators are always men, by the way, so we can assume a case of childbirth envy. Added to this is a shocking contempt for the body, which is in the tradition of Christianity; for example, Hans Moravec of Carnegie Mellon University has referred to people as "meat machines" and "baloney". From here it is only one small step towards finally ridding the earth of these disgusting flawed bodies and entering a post-human age. According to the late Marvin Minsky, who was professor at the Media Lab of the famous Massachusetts Institute of Technology in Boston when he made the remark, *people could be grateful if the robots of the future were to keep them as pets.*

Such statements are indeed made by professors at top American universities and printed by the most respected publishers. Yet how can such a scenario be enthusiastically anticipated and the attendant research funded with countless millions. The only plausible explanations are blindness or boundless self-loathing: *my own products are so magnificent, they put me so utterly to shame that I gladly submit to them.* As early as 1956, Günther Anders analysed these complex ego dynamics very astutely as "Promethean shame": today's Prometheus feels like the court dwarf in his own machine park. So it's a matter of both the immense pride in having made such fantastic machines and the crushing shame of not being able to keep up with them. In this psychological melee, you might prefer to hand over control to the robots and believe that you live on in them, your "mind children", as Moravec himself puts it.

Yes, that is an inhuman image of man. Joseph Weizenbaum, himself an important pioneer of artificial intelligence, sharply attacks this position and speaks of it as the "final solution to the human question". Having experienced the National Socialists' contempt for human beings firsthand, he sees parallels here. In any case, the question must always be asked in whose interest such an increase in performance, such an enhancement, is undertaken. Not only is this *not* about the human being, but in some cases it is even explicitly *against* it. Not everything that falls under the term transhumanism is so extreme, but a belief in the technological improvement of humans is common to all transhumanists. What is the end that justifies such means? Who defines this increase in performance and how is it defined? What is it for and who is it for, what is its use? And what is the use of utility? It is important to counteract technology's increasing independence with our minds – by thinking poetically.

Perhaps such extreme positions in the USA can also be explained by the fact that one must take a stand there in debates that seem very alien to western Europe. In America, religion, especially Christianity, plays a much more important role than in western Europe. So-called creationism is so influential in some states that evolution is not allowed to be taught in schools because it contradicts the biblical version of genesis. Against this background, it is easier to understand why such social forces are vehemently opposed by the enlightened side. At the other extreme is a scientism with purely rational and scientific argumentation structures. The result is a debating situation with two radical standpoints – and never the twain shall meet. Both are wrong and mutually reinforcing. It's like the Cold War, in which the existence of the evil other justified one's own ban on thinking.

But such harmful demarcations also exist within the sciences, between the humanities and the natural sciences, for example, and above all between the sciences and other worlds of knowledge, such as the arts. The latter have infinitely much to add to the knowledge of man; indeed, without them no knowledge of human nature is imaginable. The knowledge developed in art and literature has always inspired science; poetic thinking is of a complexity that goes beyond conceptual rationality and is used time and again for theoretical modelling. Poetic thinking is essential to avoid the danger of denying complexity.

6 Life science and form of life

"There are more things in heaven and earth, Horatio, than are dreamt of in your philosophy", as Hamlet knew. In our pragmacentric, disturbed consciousness, we must not lose sight of the actually existing unknown. Human existence should retain a dimension of the mysterious to avoid becoming finite. In the finite, the infinite must open up again and again – it has to be allowed a space in human existence to make the meaning of being human possible. A fundamental openness of spirit, i.e. more than what can be grasped by any given rationality, keeps what is human alive, since it enables a higher concept of the self. In the past, religion was responsible for this more-than-rationality and the much-discussed return of religion today indicates that our culture of knowledge with its pride in knowledge and ability does not satisfy people.

But do we really want religion to return? We should not lose the achievements and the basic liberating potential of the enlightened spirit. The problem has of course never been the enlightened spirit as such, but that instead of an enlightened concept of education, we have an economically oriented concept of ability and instrumentalised reason. Education in the sense of becoming human, the development of body, mind and soul, simply does not "pay off" in this system. Poetic thinking, on the other hand, brings to the fore a dimension that surpasses pragmacentrism and allows us to transcend our knowledge and abilities. Such a dimension of being human that goes beyond what is feasible must be maintained as potential, since otherwise we cannot justify moral and thus ethical and social values.

DOI: 10.4324/9781003367703-6

Everyone should be readily able to understand the value of the poetic in everyday life, since we have all experienced "poetic" moments, even if we don't set much store by them today. In being moved by natural beauty, in the fascination of the experience of art, in the experience of love and in the penetrating moment that consumes us, i.e. in the true encounter of the gaze of another person, we have all experienced that being human can suddenly expand infinitely and go beyond the functional context of life. This is where the integration of the poetic into our lives begins. This experience should be taken into account as such in our ideas about real life. It should be taken seriously and included in our views of the way we want to live. We have to develop opportunities to support the capacity for talking about it, for developing an awareness of it, less in the form of kitsch and bad art and more in the form of creating theories about life: in the *life sciences*.

Now, the term *life sciences* is very problematic, first of all because it is already established in the English-speaking world, where it unfortunately denotes a purely scientific approach and has little to do with the form of life. Even if literary scholars call into question this supposed monopoly the life sciences have on knowledge about human life, it can hardly be denied that the knowledge the humanities have about human life is marginalised in the power structures of our society. These literary life sciences are neither funded nor listened to. Yet they can provide answers to questions on which the natural sciences have absolutely nothing to say, such as the pressing question in our global world of how different cultures might live together.

The literary sciences will, however, hardly be able to assert themselves against the already established idea of life sciences if they claim the term life sciences for themselves. In any case, the literary, and therefore also the poetic, is not limited to its – undoubtedly considerable – sociological analytical skills.

From the point of view of poetic thinking, I therefore propose to speak of *disciplines of meaning* because this makes clear the difference between factual knowledge and what one does with it. Facts require interpretation, classification in historical contexts, i.e. in culturally and individually determined worldviews. A fact by itself means nothing, it makes no sense. It can be understood and interpreted in completely contradictory ways, as anyone who has ever argued knows: mostly it is about how a concrete action is to be understood. Although both parties to the argument have experienced the fact, depending on the perspective, opinions about what happened differ – the same thing can evidently be experienced in completely different ways. Everything, every phenomenon of the human world, acquires sense or meaning only historically, culturally and subjectively.

The life sciences can therefore say nothing about meaning, which also means that life is devoid of meaning if the natural sciences are viewed as life sciences, since all possible subjective and historically conditioned interpretations are disregarded. Of course, scientific knowledge helps shape these possibilities, but the notion that they alone should determine them can at best be described as naïve.

So if we want to be clear about the importance of facts, including – but by no means only – scientific facts for society, for individuals and for human life, we need theories that provide information about the processes involved in the creation of meaning. Language is essential in allowing phenomena of all kinds that are perceived with the senses to be processed in the mind, understood and thus translated into a worldview. In language, people develop their view of the world. This always happens in exchange with other people, whether directly or indirectly – this is the core of the cultural process. Of course, this also takes place within the natural sciences. In the poetic, though, the central question is how meaning arises in the first place. That is why poetic thinking is so crucial in the intellectual context of today: it represents the basis for a holistic understanding of the processes by which meaning is created.

If we want to think poetically, that is, humanly, then we must first see what we even mean by human life. In Greek there is a distinction between *zoë* and *bios*. According to Giorgio Agamben, *zoë* denotes the simple state of being alive, it is mere life, considered as detached from the circumstances and concrete form of being in this life. *Bios*, on the other hand, considers life in unity with its life form, its environment. Although the ancient Greeks did not necessarily make this clear division, it is interesting and helpful as a figure of thought.

Politics has the task of organising public life, creating infrastructure and establishing general rules. It is understandable that it tends to disregard individual life and pursue the interests of the general public. In the past, the ruling power was mainly limited to killing political opponents and criminals who violated the established rules, but otherwise letting people live. So it was mainly concerned with punishing dangerous bodies. However, with the increasing prevalence of liberal economic models, especially from the early nineteenth century onwards, the form of rule shifted in favour of an understanding of politics in which the ruling power makes people live and lets them die. The focus was no longer so much on protecting against dangers, but on regulating the population. In addition to the judiciary and the military, politics has now taken over concern for the form of life of the population.

In the name of this new area of political activity, well-meaning intentions regarding how life should be upgraded have been pursued. Everyone was to be given the opportunity to lead a good, secure life. Hygiene measures were introduced and the education system was developed, which could, while delivering basic knowledge, consolidate concepts of sexuality and morality. Life in all its aspects was supervised and regulated by the state. This is what Michel Foucault called *biopolitics* (although the term had always been used in various ways and still is). Living conditions were in many respects improved enormously, as already noted, but at the same time the possibility of viewing the population primarily as an element of economic calculation arose.

So the intention behind these measures was not necessarily, or at least not only, to make people's lives more liveable, it was about shaping a population that would be able to produce on command and increase the power and interest of the rulers. As a result, this approach could also be turned around: instead of upgrading life, it was possible to shift the focus to opposing "degraded" life. And not because it affects safety, but simply because it supposedly reduces the life of the population in general. The population is to be kept physically and morally healthy or pure, so disturbing elements must be eliminated lest the body politic be infested. This meant an individual could be killed to safeguard a desired development within the population.

As we can see, biopolitics always includes the danger of regulating life, which means people are no longer regarded as unique individuals, but only in terms of their function in the big picture. That brings a reification of the human being.

Nazism was obviously a culmination of this form of biopolitics, but the attitude was widespread as early as the nineteenth century and took many other dreadful forms in the twentieth. Stalinism, the Khmer Rouge, the Chinese Cultural Revolution are just a few other examples of the madness that ensues as soon as the "body of the nation" acquires a higher value than the individual. Hitler saw himself as an artist, as a sculptor of the body of the people, which he wanted to chisel according to his own ideas so as to perfect it. There was plenty of idealism at work there – but unfortunately of a completely perverted kind.

To a certain extent, politics of course must set out to educate and form the people – and the term should be understood in the broadest sense. However, this must never go hand in hand with fighting those who think differently – it must always allow scope for different forms of living. There must be no drawing of boundaries between a life worth living and a life not worth living. Politics must never succumb outright to biopolitics. To do so means becoming totalitarian. The matter needs formulating: politics should not form the people itself but should rather provide them with every opportunity to cultivate themselves.

Our era offers more opportunities for biopolitics than ever. We have developed technologies and infrastructure that can enforce regulatory measures better and more comprehensively than ever before. At the same time, fortunately, we have also developed our means of self-analysis. In addition to the objectifying processes of biopolitics, modernity has also developed subjectifying techniques of the self. The arts belong to these processes that strengthen subjectivity. If we want to oppose biopolitics, we have to think poetically.

If we think poetically we can never think of life only as *zoë*, as mere life. Poetic thinking always thinks of human life with its form, it never separates *zoë* from *bios*. Human life is therefore always a possibility of life, it can never be reduced to its facticity. Man is a being of possibility.

When classifying living beings, the great biologist Carl von Linné initially did not call the human being *homo sapiens* but rather *homo nosce te ipsum*, meaning "human recognise thyself". To grasp the uniqueness of the human in an imperative is a very nice idea. It makes it clear that what is human consists of a process that is never complete. The human is never finally achieved but can only be striven for time and again. This also means that we can only speak of the human as a claim. It is a demand on ourselves. What is special about being human is a potential that is accessible to everyone, but which is only ever reached in certain moments. A *potentialist anthropology* emerges here: the human is no longer defined by something that is, but by a possibility and a claim.

If we see the human being as a possibility, as a potential that we should always strive towards, the question arises as to how this potential can be realised and, above all, what it looks like. What should we in fact be striving for?

There is a difference between being exceptionally good at a computer game and developing an idea or technology that will help millions of people to suffer less. At the very least, those achievements should not be awarded the same social recognition. To paint a picture or write a book that brings clarity and consciousness to a problem of our time, maybe even providing a perspective for dealing with it, should garner the highest recognition our society has to offer. Pushing the boundaries of our consciousness, even when there is no obvious use value involved, as is often the case in the arts, is an infinitely valuable achievement for humanity. Recognition is, however, often absent or minimal, particularly when the form is too new or too complex, or it comes only after a long wait, often when the artist is dead.

Where athletes and pop musicians are concerned it's quite another story. They have become the gods of our society, stars soaring above all earthly beings. Whereas "intellectual" is a dirty word, a tennis coach is treated with the utmost respect. While university professors in the humanities in most countries today can only modestly support a family on their salary, top football players earn many times as much – and squander a few professors' monthly salaries in one evening without batting an eyelid. Entertainment for the masses has become the highest value because, in the logic of the economy, it is the most profitable. Likewise, hedge fund managers can feel validated by their "earnings". No matter how much people talk about "products" in the financial world, they don't "produce" anything and very often their work does nothing to promote the interest of society as a whole. One only needs to look at their severance packages to see that if they just stop working and do no further damage it is worth many millions. As early as the eighteenth century, Lichtenberg established that it is people with middle incomes who carry society. But these middle classes are shrinking.

Of course, these conditions serve only to promote the high earners' megalomania. The system makes it clear via the income distribution that they have nothing to do with normal mortals and that such small fry, whose annual income they can "earn" in a couple of hours, are worth nothing in comparison to them. And even a humanities scholar, a university lecturer and perhaps someone highly educated and of international renown in their specialist field cannot be taken seriously according to the economic logic and scale of recognition. Trump prides himself on being able to grab every woman between the legs on account of his wealth. For him, leaving aside all considerations of the divisions of the sexes, human value is defined purely economically. Mass compatibility must not be the decisive criterion. Income levels are certainly a point at which politics could begin with a view to pushing through values that promote society.

There is no question that top athletes achieve amazing things, and that should be rewarded. Unfortunately, they seem to inspire very few in their audience to try as hard as they do. For most fans, whose interest generates the athletes' income, the stimulus translates merely to drinking beer and munching crisps. In the most unfortunate cases we can add the physical activity of punch-ups and rioting. Nonetheless, sport is accepted as an area in which people can appreciate achievement and grace. What is usually looked at askance is still celebrated here: elegance.

So it's about the big question of what values we have and cultivate. How do we define what is desirable? What kinds of performance should be funded? And how can we support those? Societal benefit is a broad concept, and of course entertainment plays its part too, as long as it doesn't convey anti-social ideas. At any rate, the expansion of the spiritual limits of mankind is part of it as well as the cultivation of this spiritual culture. So we have to develop attitudes and mechanisms to recognise these spiritual achievements.

Until recently, written culture was responsible for cultivating and securing such values. Humanistic culture and its values were built on the written word, and literature was the key medium in which such values were negotiated. Some time ago, however, literature lost this role. It was replaced by television, film and the internet, with the result that the whole value system is in flux and there is uncertainty. So far, these new media have not been able to take on the role of literature. They may have power, but they affect the nation differently. This is perhaps due to their seductiveness for a passive reception. They typically demand less than literature.

There is always a range of different factors that affect people and vie for their attention. On the one hand, there are social and cultural practices that are intended to tame people's passions and drives, and to convert their energies into socially acceptable and beneficial activities, i.e. to make them socially skilled. On the other hand, there are factors that strengthen people in their drives and lusts and that leave aside consideration for others. The new media quite often have a bestialising effect. The internet and entertainment culture primarily appeal to people's most primitive instincts. Pornography and the glorification of violence are seeing an unprecedented upswing with these media. These bestialising tendencies must be controlled and limited if society is to survive. Humans must cultivate themselves so as not to be drowned in chaos and violence. We have to make rules for ourselves.

In this context, Peter Sloterdijk speaks of *anthropotechnics*. That is, humans create themselves; there are techniques for this human production. Care must be taken to limit techniques that strengthen the bestialising aspects and to encourage techniques that strengthen the socially productive aspects. Humans must therefore work towards their refinement and spiritualisation. Here, too, the problem is that the state cannot and must not enforce a repressive cultural policy. These aims must be promoted in other ways. Once again, the starting point must be the individual, who, of their own free will, must be willing to think beyond comfort and cultivate concern for the self. It boils down once more to education and cultural guiding principles.

As self-creating beings, humans have always developed training systems to improve and expand their abilities – physical and mental exercises. Through such self-forming and self-enhancing behaviours, humans cultivate themselves. Ignatius of Loyola spoke of *exercitia spiritualia*, Sloterdijk suggested the term *asceticism* for it – both terms are simply foreign language expressions for exercise. Michel Foucault's late work is likewise dedicated to the study of such exercise systems, especially in relation to sexuality. There, they are called *souci de soi*, concern for the self, which also means technologies for self-definition and self-enhancement.

Far from being just about physical dexterity or an efficient use of tools, such training involves mental exercises that are at least as important since it is precisely the latter that motivate great achievements in the first place. So it is above all moral and idealistic notions, asceticism in the more classical sense, i.e. renunciation of pleasure in favour of spiritual values, that have produced the important cultural achievements. The entire cultural heritage of mankind builds on such renunciation and orientation towards the spiritual, as well as everything that makes up human life, namely the values underpinning the life of our relationships. The differences between people and cultures are based on different exercises and their more or less diligent practice. Exercise is therefore crucial for individual and societal development.

If, however, in our time, perplexity about criteria of values prevails, then higher goals can no longer be formulated and all manner of exercise systems push their way onto the market. In this scenario, everything is measured by economic success, the ultimate criterion being mass participation. The more people like something, the better it is. This state of affairs leads to a general levelling out, since anything extraordinary cannot be good by these standards. It can only be better within the framework of the ordinary. Anything that really excels gets no recognition. Sloterdijk calls this the loss of *vertical tension*. All vertical difference, in which outstanding achievements are recognised, is converted into horizontal difference, so only the masses count, and of course they only feel addressed by what is suited to them.

This is a fundamental problem of democracy, of which it is being said increasingly openly these days that it has failed. That is the wrong approach, however. A democracy can obviously only be as good as the population that constitutes it. That is why it must do everything in its power to make or keep its population democratically capable. This means that the vast majority of people living in a democracy must recognise the value of self-cultivation, both physical and mental. Included in this is the quantitatively non-measurable performance that is cultivated in inwardness and contemplation. It expresses itself in humanistic and creative ideals that must be supported by a spiritually oriented education system. Forms of practising life that oppose coarseness must be developed and cultivated. If democracy fails in this, it will collapse as a system, it will be endangered and dangerous.

We have already addressed the connection with contemporary technologies: if self-improvement is no longer achieved through practice and ascesis, but is accessed as a biotechnical and surgical service, the comfort-seeking ego is relieved and pampered, but at the same time self-creation is handed over to external authorities. This leads to dependence on technology and consequently dependence on the owners of the various technologies. In addition, the will to make an effort suffers, so essential aspects of the human psyche atrophy. In addition, corporations and states have unforeseeable opportunities to steer people's wishes and opinions by means of big data, social media and control mechanisms. It is becoming increasingly difficult to resist such manipulations, which mostly serve particular interests. The result is the rug is pulled out from under the feet of any desirable form of individual or social development.

What is particularly interesting about all these efforts and findings is that we have now evidently reached a new phase of postmodernism, if we wish to use this unfortunate expression at all – which I would like to do here as a concession to convention. Postmodernism has brought difference and alterity to the fore, thereby breaking with rigid and outdated ideas. However, the consequence is not the notorious "postmodern relativism", as was long believed, but the inescapable necessity of cultivation. That assigns enormous importance and responsibility to the disciplines of meaning.

7 Attitude, mood, atmosphere

You can't practise poetic thinking because it's simply not a technique. It's a thinking mode that you can only jump into. But you can instead practise an attitude or a readiness that better enables you to get into that mode. Only the poetic mood allows poetic perception, as Novalis already claimed in Romanticism. So we can only perceive whatever we allow, whatever has a place in our world. In this respect we must give the poetic such a place so that it can take place. Poetic thinking must be cultivated as a life plan to create the conditions for the poetic.

Our culture suffers from the fact that it can hardly name what is most fundamental to human life, namely the *atmospheres* in which we move and of which we are a part. Only the most primitive terms and forms of expression are available to us to locate ourselves symbolically in our being-in-relationship. Here the extent of the difficulty already becomes clear: there is no expression even for the fact that our being is essentially determined by relationships. If you attempt to address these matters, you inevitably sound muddle-headed. Even literature has now largely quit trying. We can hardly get beyond the banal distinction between a good and a bad atmosphere.

So there is a blatant contrast between our true experience of life and our means of expression. That is, however, not due to a supposedly fundamental deficiency in language, but to our deficient culture, which has not formed any expressions for it. This is a problem because this condition alienates us from ourselves. What's more, and this only adds to the problem, this area is dominated by kitsch. It has been left to kitsch. Art hardly dares to approach it

DOI: 10.4324/9781003367703-7

anymore, yet art bears the responsibility here. So our society needs an expansion in and beyond the domain of art, an increase in language, expression and awareness, if it does not want to let the state of being human wither.

Conventional scientific terminology cannot cover these areas either, which is why science swiftly dismisses them as irrelevant. Yet they do exist, so much so that it has to be said that all human beings are determined by atmospheres and have an atmosphere themselves. In this regard, too, it makes sense to consider ourselves as embodied rather than merely as beings that have a body, because as embodied, as a mind-body unit, these effects admit of thought more easily. We not only have an influence on our environment by means of our words and gestures, but our whole being radiates. It is said that fear can be "smelled", a "radiant" person acts like sunshine and spreads light and warmth, while another person "sends shivers down your spine". These are figures of speech that testify to the noticeable spatial effect of a human mood. We can leave all this to esoterical aura researchers, yet it would be better to develop rational approaches to such phenomena as far as possible and to make the latter capable of being rendered in scientific language.

When atmosphere is spoken of in aesthetic contexts, it is always a matter of expressing something that is difficult to say, something that is beyond what can be rationally verified. So it's merely a sign of our own speechlessness. Walter Benjamin tried to investigate the atmospheric with his concept of aura. Actually, what is aesthetically relevant lies precisely in the atmosphere, because aesthetics is the study of perception. So when aesthetics go beyond purely physical contexts, it always has to do with atmosphere.

Interestingly, politicians and economists assign a major role to atmosphere. In negotiations, for instance, much is done to create a good atmosphere and put the negotiating partner in the right mood. No expense is spared because the deal or political agreement depends on the feel of the situation. In fact, in general, most verbal communication serves to actualise atmosphere. The whole notion of small talk consists exclusively of enlivening the atmosphere. Someone who only ever talked to the point would be so unpleasant as to have a slim chance of being listened to.

The term "atmosphere" comes from the Greek and can be translated as "sphere of influence". So it's about something coming to the fore, emerging characteristically and having an effect. Gernot Böhme, who had tried to bring the term atmosphere into the scientific sphere for some time, speaks of "ecstasies of the thing". A thing radiates into its surroundings and becomes perceptible in space. It thus acquires forms of presence that go beyond the simple displacement of space by a body.

If this radiating presence is created through the tangible presence of things, then this means that a connection between object and subject obtains. This is exciting because it means that thinking in terms of the atmospheric dissolves the fundamental western subject-object separation. When we no longer have this separation, our entire conception of the ego is overthrown. Little wonder western science can't deal with it and doesn't even want to.

It cannot be denied, however: in perceiving the atmosphere we explode the object status of what is perceived. Together with the entire environment and with the perceiving subject, objects form a multiple overlapping space. Perception, reality and the world are constituted only in this common reality of the atmosphere. Perceiving therefore means being effective, genuinely being. The German terms are instructive here: perception, "Wahrnehmung", literally gives us "Wahr-Nehmung", "true-taking" or taking what is true, and "Wirklich-Sein", "actually-being", means genuinely being, with a sense also of being effective, as "wirken" means to have an effect, to be effective.

We can only perceive when we are in our surroundings. Meaning always appears in context. Everything must first be integrated in the human-constituted world to be able to take on meaning in this context. Without a reference context there is no meaning and no world.

So when it comes to the atmospheric, we are dealing with relational thinking – we will return to this in detail in connection with the dialogical. However, to think of the relationship itself rather than just the objects, a certain attitude is required. We must pay attention to that. We must also behave in a manner that is self-restrained, i.e. not taking over all the space for ourselves, but rather allowing room for development. Relationships as such are not controllable, one must let them be, allow them their existence. It's ultimately akin to art: if we want to have an art experience, we shouldn't want to grab the art, we have to let it grab us. In this respect, art is important training and cultivation for poetic thinking.

Atmospheres can of course be created linguistically, but they also exist pre-linguistically. You walk into a room and immediately perceive the atmosphere – without any need for words. However, it must be added that, strictly speaking, there is nothing pre-linguistic in the human world, since it is only through our symbolic forms, all of which ultimately amount to language, that we create a world and an I, world understood as a spiritually permeated world. Everything is then integrated into this framework. So if something exists without language – and of course that is possible, we are also bodily beings – then it is grasped mentally only on the basis of what has already been achieved in language. Things exist for themselves but humans need to integrate them into their world, and this happens in language. This process shapes their perception. But we will return also to language thinking in more detail in a moment. The idea here was to suggest this connection briefly before discussing the concept of immanent transcendence, which is helpful in the context of thinking about atmosphere and relationship.

8 Immanent transcendence, silence and presence

Transcendence is often wrongly understood as a solely religious term, more or less as a synonym for metaphysics. However, it is also possible to understand the term in a thoroughly earthly way. Transcendence literally means "that which goes beyond". So what goes beyond the given can very well have its roots in the given and take its impetus from there. Nietzsche already wanted to base transcendence on human life. Man's transcendence lies within man's being; it is based on the senses. Accordingly, we can speak of an *immanent transcendence*. Nietzsche's notoriously misused term "the superman" is based on this. The superman is precisely this claim to surpassing oneself; being human consists precisely in this upward striving. Ultimately, therefore, man is not left behind by the superman at all, rather the dimension of the superman is precisely what is decisive about being human. Here too my concept of a potentialist anthropology is apt: if man is not reduced to a physical anthropology, then we are necessarily dealing with a potentialist anthropology. The spiritual part is always potentialistic.

With this idea of transcendence, the meaning of life does not lie outside the realm of human life; this transcendence is immanent. Human beings give their meaning to themselves, out of themselves. In this way life justifies itself aesthetically, as Nietzsche said. If you understand the human by way of the question "What is the human?" and if this question always points beyond the human and includes its potentiality, the human being becomes transcendent itself. It realises its being precisely when it transcends itself. It is precisely in transcending that humans actualise and realise themselves.

DOI: 10.4324/9781003367703-8

Even if this idea does not proceed from a metaphysical entity, but from our earthly present, there is of course a proximity, if not to religion, then to mysticism. Everyone has experienced moments in which the unity or connection of being has dawned on them. However, this is difficult to accept in our analytical culture. The more analytical our mind, the more resistance it will put up against such moments. Our great analytical awareness also creates areas of lack of awareness – which of course cannot be perceived as such by analytical thinking. What is blocked out is the very fact that everyone's foundation is this unity with the rest of the world. As babies, we were beings that were hardly separated at all from the rest of the world. Even as small children, the unity we formed with our mothers was difficult to break, and we achieved subject-object separation, in other words self-awareness, only by means of immense effort and a great deal of suffering.

The more we have trained ourselves analytically, the more difficult it seems to be to overcome this sense of disconnection and re-enter that "oceanic feeling", as Freud put it, using a term borrowed from Romain Rolland. Yet this possibility exists for us: everything that we call enthusiasm falls into this category. Love, art, closeness to nature, a true human encounter are all ways to enter this state, which is certainly closely related to the mystical state.

If we think about how we perceive the world, that is, if we practise aesthetics, the study of perception, *aisthesis*, then it is difficult to do entirely without mystical elements. Aesthetic experience shares an eventful time structure with mystical experience. We have stepped out of the temporal sequence of events and are in the here and now. Time no longer consists of measurable units, but is both momentary and eternal, we are suspended in the moment of the event. As a result, the experience also has something ecstatic about it – we have stepped out of the everyday context of action and are amazed. This also means that our own actions have become receptive and passive, we stand in the flow of things instead of directing them in a goal-oriented manner. Our own clear boundaries as subjects acting and influencing the objects have dissolved, instead the categories of subject and object merge and we are absorbed in this larger whole. This then leads to a serenity, one might also call it security in being.

Such an eventful mode of experience always seems to contain something of the *unio mystica*, i.e. the feeling of mystical unity with the world. When one perceives aesthetically, when one really becomes aware of something and thus partakes of its truth, one is connected with what is perceived. Obviously, such a *unio mystica* cannot be brought about in a planned manner; one has to be relaxed or serene, to keep oneself in a state in which one can be grasped instead of wanting to grasp things oneself. It is event, revelation, *hic et nunc*. As such, it explodes our thought structures. We cannot fully grasp such an experience with our thinking, accordingly we cannot describe it exhaustively either, but only ever approach it and circle it in order to give it a place in our conception of life – and even if it is only a blank space, better: a free space. That is poetic thinking.

Silence does the most justice to this circumstance. That's why there exists a highly charged silence, more eloquent and powerful than words and action. The notion of a "roaring silence" speaks to such an experience. Of course, such silence must be staged. Charismatic people can turn silence into powerful action through gestures, facial expressions and, above all, through sudden interruptions and pauses. Such silence has performative power. It makes a cut, time is suspended and you are in the present, at a crossroads where everything can tip over and decisive things happen. This pausing is also an awareness and thus a concentrating on the self. You are thrown back on yourself, you cannot cling to external things for distraction. You are forced to be in the here and now, in the present. Such moments of presence are always instances of intense being, in which you don't escape from yourself.

Of course, silence can also be part of speech, and it is no coincidence that the most eloquent and deepest poets have made silence an essential part of their poetic ideas. In poetry, the crucial things often happen between the words, in the white spaces of the text. Enjambements, breaking up the sentence structure, breaking off the word – such techniques make silence audible. The clearest, or at least the most diagrammatic example of expressive silence is Eugen Gomringer's poem *Silence*:

silence silence silence
silence silence silence
silence   silence
silence silence silence
silence silence silence

The silence is only there where it is not – the meaning of the word only really appears in the open space.

Silence is an atmospheric phenomenon. Our perceptual schema is suspended since we have no object that can be perceived and since the subject steps outside itself. This stepping outside the usual subject-object scheme, this ecstasy, is mystical. It conveys a sense of connection – of truth. A certain willingness to let go, surrender and lose, makes it easier to enter this state. Serenity. Otherwise, we arm ourselves against this kind of experience, which actually has something terrifying about it, since we're out of control, at the mercy of being, for good or ill. That's a big risk, we don't like it, we, the self-determined, who rule over our lives and the world. Ruling is also a defence against being overwhelmed. Sometimes, however, we are simply taken by surprise, sometimes by a very delicate force.

So the correct attitude is part of poetic thinking but it's not an absolute requirement as life at times proves stronger anyway. Poetic thinking has a paradoxical structure because it deals conceptually with the realm of human existence that perforce eludes the conceptual and that concepts cannot get a handle on. It is about the conceptualisation of immediate experience, about the intelligibility of presence.

Yet how can presence be consciously perceived? Presence is precisely the unmediated, that which is not already mentally processed and made conscious in this processing. Through such mental processing, something acquires meaning but loses its presence. Sense and presence are inevitably in conflict with each other. Things can sometimes assert a kind of executive truth: they simply are. Against this being, however, we as human beings must build a world. It's not the case that we simply are, rather, we are always *becoming* in symbolic processes.

The present tears open time, tears us and what we perceive out of our routine and places us in a context. Breaking apart the automatisms is a basic requirement of every perception. The present is always new, always unique. Presence is the sense of connection of the self with the whole. It reveals itself in mysticism.

The eternal need for presence has gone out of fashion in western culture. Once the mediality of all experience, the shift between being and thinking, had become clear, nobody wanted to speak of presence anymore. But in recent years, this need has returned with a vengeance. Living without presence is not good – for all our realisations of our limitations, we now realise that we need to develop concepts to include presence in our ideas of ourselves and of how we live – and how we want to live. Despite all its breathtaking achievements, our knowledge system has, like all knowledge, developed a special form of ignorance. Anything that doesn't fit into the analytical logic of the system is simply pushed aside. This makes it almost impossible to become aware of blind spots. Presence is one of those things we can't think today. It requires a different theory of language, which we will discuss later.

We have also noticed that we are bodies, and this being thrown back onto our bodily being represents a counterbalance to the attribution of meaning. We must therefore ideally live both at the same time: meaningfulness and presence. Attributing meaning, a process which is always deferred, and the immediate being of presence – both of these effects should flutter in us like the flag of life in the wind.

In every experience of the world there are components of meaning and of presence, as Hans Ulrich Gumbrecht has pointed out. Yet in western culture today, the aspect of meaning has become more dominant than ever. We no longer let the world get to us and have trained the way we experience so that everything we perceive is mediated by an interpretive approach. But the aspect of presence cannot be completely ignored and has been finding its way back into our culture for some time. Two areas in which this is clearly underway are sports and the arts. It is obvious that the growing need for presence is manifesting itself primarily through the body, for instance in drug use, bodybuilding, all kinds of extreme sports – bungee jumping is probably the best example – but also the individual's experience of mass sport events or rock concerts. I have already mentioned the problems that arise when it is body thinking rather than embodied thinking that is behind these phenomena. That entails an even greater objectification of the body, or at the very least a further separation of body and mind, which can lead to abuse and manifest itself in violence, oppression, nationalism and racism. Nonetheless, this same tendency contains also the potential to cultivate, by way of the body, an awareness of our embodiedness and a kind of thinking that involves presence.

Ultimately, some way of mediating between presence and meaning must be found: a way of thinking that does not block out presence. This is what poetic thinking strives for. Hans Ulrich Gumbrecht recognises this important contemporary phenomenon, drawing our attention to the significance of epiphanies, moments of intensity and aesthetic experience. The separation of the spheres of presence and meaning has yet to be overcome, however. The concepts of meaning must be expanded. Even in the most immediate experience, that which has the quality of an event, presence must be thought of together with meaning – indeed, such an experience must first be thinkable. Gumbrecht quotes an athlete who describes the fascination of competitive sport as "losing yourself in focused intensity". In doing so, he refers to the necessary oscillation and tension between the effects of presence and meaning. Aesthetic experience makes it possible to experience the components of meaning and presence in their tension. Such is the approach of poetic thinking, with the aim of allowing human beings to be holistically in tune with the things of the world.

The poetic in art is a means of producing presence. A work of art breaks with the usual notions of presence and absence, showing us things that previously lay outside the realm of possibility. With such eventfulness, they invade time and stand for the moment in it. They also present presence. Art thinks the context of presence. Without art this cannot be thought. It is the poetic aspect of art that accomplishes this feat. This correspondence of meaning and presence is given precisely in poetry; as a form of language it is both sound and silence, arrangement and processing, sensual perception and symbolic form, as well as the attribution of meaning, which takes place primarily through its form. This is exactly what poetic thinking means.

9 Thinking language

Language thinking is a prerequisite for poetic thinking, if only because all thinking, as a mental processing of the world, must ultimately proceed through language. Language thinking is based on the knowledge that our sense-making access to the world is linguistic. In any case, our idea of language shapes our understanding of the world and of being. But thinking language is not just a theory, it is an activity: it is the very process of this specific thinking.

Language thinking represents a historical anthropology of language. In other words, language is fundamental to being human, and language and being human are historically and culturally conditioned. I have already criticised one-sided biologism for neglecting precisely those dimensions, historicity and culture. The same goes for naturalistic and universalistic ideas. They usually have very well-meaning intentions, they aim for equality for all people, and I certainly subscribe to that. However, this goal must be achieved in a different way, because these ideas are not a pertinent description of the human being. We humans are what we make of ourselves – in this respect we cannot ignore the historicity of how we are constituted. Our conception of language must also take into account the historical, the culturally particular and the unique.

The great language thinker Wilhelm von Humboldt described language as an invitation to "understand through thinking together" instead of – at best – "acting through empathy". According to Humboldt, only humans have such a language. Animals can prompt action as humans can, arouse and convey feelings, but human language has something that goes beyond the language of animals. In the following I want to explain this essential surplus, which I call the poetic.

It is already clear from Humboldt's quote that this poetic element is by no means just a matter of feeling. As I said, animals have feelings too, there can be no doubt about that – yet I wouldn't concede the poetic aspect to them. But how does the poetic go beyond feelings? Poetic thinking is ultimately also an effort to *think feelings*.

Understanding through thinking together means that cognition and communication go together: thinking and mediation coincide here. This gives language a tremendous role and one that is difficult for us in our European, i.e. generally western, tradition to grasp. We operate in a two-and-a-half-thousand-year-old tradition that is very critical of language. Although hardly anyone denies its importance today, it is mostly cursed: most people think that life and the world would be much easier to manage without the peculiarities of language. Let's be honest: don't we often rail against language for defying us and simply not wanting to express what's going on with us?

Well, from the standpoint of poetic thinking, that's a mistake. We may have inklings of areas of being that elude us, but these areas only exist through language. If we cannot grasp them in language, we must not lay that at the door of language, it's rather our world that is not sufficiently developed. "The limits of my language mean the limits of my world", said Ludwig Wittgenstein quite rightly. We build our world for ourselves in a mental processing of it, and for that mental processing we are dependent on language.

However, our European culture has mostly seen it very differently and this powerful tradition still has a strong impact on our ideas. We are all heirs of Greek philosophy, and Plato wanted to think without language, or so he pretended, at least. In his texts he did indeed work on language and with his dialogues he wrote what are more or less mini-plays. So he was by no means a "language-neutral" philosopher – which is an impossibility anyway, even if many philosophers have striven for it.

Plato believed in ideas that exist in their own right and to which we have only mediated access. For him, language is an additional intermediate step. It removes us even farther from the ideas – in this respect it comes off badly in his work. Aristotle cemented this separation of thought and language. According to him, people first think something and only then add words to express what they have thought. So in his view our thinking, cognition, would be possible without language. Language would then be for communication only. And even if intellectual history has long since said goodbye to such ideas, hand on heart, who doesn't find themselves leaning on it from time to time? *I know it, I just can't express it –* this sentence is an expression of this outdated theory of language. *I know there is still something to know, but I can't think of it yet because I haven't developed my language enough* – that would be a correct version of it. Such an awareness of lack, the acknowledgement of one's own limitations, is actually the first step towards being able to think what has not yet been born. In that case, I am the one who hasn't developed my language, and thus my world and my consciousness of the world, enough. Holding language fundamentally responsible for this, on the other hand, obstructs the possibility of thinking.

In addition to Greek philosophy, the Christian religion, which developed from it, became the cornerstone of our history of ideas. Unfortunately, language doesn't fare any better as a result. It does say in the Bible, in the Gospel of John, *In the beginning was the word*, but we are already assuming a translation into Greek here in our English translation, and the Greek expression *logos* is heavily in need of – and dependent on – interpretation. Goethe immortalised this difficulty in Faust's study monologue:

> 'Tis written: "In the beginning was the Word!"
> Here now I'm balked! Who'll put me in accord?
> It is impossible, the *Word* so high to prize,
> I must translate it otherwise
> If I am rightly by the Spirit taught.
> 'Tis written: In the beginning was the *Thought!*
> Consider well that line, the first you see,
> That your pen may not write too hastily!
> Is it then *Thought* that works, creative, hour by hour?
> Thus should it stand: In the beginning was the *Power!*
> Yet even while I write this word, I falter,

For something warns me, this too I shall alter.
The Spirit's helping me! I see now what I need
And write assured: In the beginning was the *Deed!*
   (Translated by George Madison Priest, 1941)

In the end, Faust decides to translate *logos* not as *word* but as *deed*. That is a crucial step in which ultimately all the problems of modernity are implicated. It explains *Faustian striving* as a will to master things in a thirst for knowledge.

But as I said, we are already dealing here with a takeover of Hebrew thought by way of the Greek spirit, since our intellectual history is based on the Greek, not the original, version of the Bible. And because of its theory of language, this Greek spirit could not really absorb the original biblical thinking. In the biblical Hebrew there is a different conception of language. It works with a highly differentiated system of hierarchical accents, so that meaning can never be located in the individual word, but only in the entire utterance, which is connected by these accents and forms a unit. I hope that by the end of this chapter it will have become clear why we should look at our European languages in the same way. Yet our culture does not usually do so.

Already in the biblical Genesis we find the view that language serves the purpose of appropriating the world: by naming, humans can become the administrators of all things on earth. Communication then leads to ruin, however. Conversation is what makes the Fall possible. On the other hand, and this is precisely the background to the Fall, humans only come to knowledge, insight and self-awareness in this way. Conversation, first between the serpent and Eve, then between Eve and Adam, leads to the desire to eat the fruit of the tree of knowledge and thereby become godlike. In fact, through language humans achieve this goal: they too become creators, conscious and creative individuals. The price to be paid is high: expulsion from paradise. The paradisiacal state would therefore be unconscious being without knowledge. Without language and conversation, humans were just animals satisfied with nature. They had no worries. It was bare being, which they long for to this day. Consciousness, i.e. language, drives us out of the paradise of unreflective and uncomplicated existence. The longing for paradise is therefore not only a wish for unity, it is also a longing for the simple, even for the spiritless life. Ultimately, humans striving for paradise wish to be animals again. This ideal should probably be reconsidered.

Today we humans are interfering with the second tree of paradise, the tree of life. We have been doing this for some time through environmental degradation, and more recently in a much more drastic way, through genetic engineering. One day we will certainly also long for the time before this second fall, when we were still denied the option of intervening in the mystery of life. The question is, however, whether the benefits we will reap from this new skill will be as tremendous as those that language brought us.

When humans, through their ability to speak and communicate, sought to usurp God's superior position by building the Tower of Babel, God realised that the penalty for their first self-empowerment was not enough. A life of toil and pain cannot stop people from wanting to become gods. To achieve that, you must go right to the root and undo the ability to communicate and the immense increases in skill and power that go with it. So, in response to the Tower of Babel, God disrupted the ability to communicate and created a multiplicity of languages.

There is, to be sure, also the story of Pentecost in the Bible, in which these communication difficulties are overcome. As soon as the Holy Spirit descends among the people, they understand each other, all the different languages suddenly become one and man is allowed to arise from his spiritual isolation for a moment and be absorbed in a feeling of unity. But apart from such moments of grace, language in the biblical tradition is in a bad way: it is synonymous with seduction and hubris, and the multiplicity of languages is a loss of the unity and original authenticity of the Adamic language.

Two instances of longing haunt European intellectual history: on the one hand, the longing for linguistic unity – diversity should not interfere with communication; on the other hand, the longing for speechless knowledge – language itself should not interfere with cognition. According to these views, the solution to all the problems of this world would be to think without language and then put our thoughts into a kind of Esperanto, a neutral uniform language, in order to communicate them to our fellow human beings. The historical languages that have evolved are real villains in this long tradition, which in various forms still prevails to this day.

Modern science, for one, clearly inscribes itself in this tradition. Scientific languages are technical languages; they have developed their own vocabulary to avoid as much as possible being infected by the vernacular, which is regarded as unclear. They want to be objective, i.e. avoid any subjective, historical and cultural colouring: pure communication of facts is required. Language is understood here as a mere means.

It was Francis Bacon, the founder of modern science, who forged the path: for him, language is a very imperfect means and must first be cleaned of incorrect use to be suitable for the communication of correct knowledge. For him, words are the "mirages of the market", which are full of the prejudices of stupid people and distort thinking. Bacon recognised, then, that language shapes thinking, but unfortunately, from his point of view, it does so in the wrong way, so science must first make language clear and correct. It is the lack of clarity that is unbearable for science. That is why it strives for objectivity and neutrality of thought, and ultimately also for a form of speechlessness.

John Locke then described language as "a mist before our eyes". Analytical thinking wants to dissolve this visual impairment. The analytical philosophy of the twentieth century, which has been able to expand its position of power enormously across universities in recent decades, is pursuing this programme further. It is true that with Ludwig Wittgenstein analytical philosophy recognised that philosophy is also linguistic and that the meaning of any word is "its use in language". But that has hardly made analytical philosophy any better disposed towards language, on the contrary: Wittgenstein spoke of the "pitfalls" of language, the mind is "bewitched" by it, thinking "gets bruises" from running up against it. It's apparent that thinking is still cast in the role of victim vis-à-vis evil language. It is still considered a matter of regret that thinking is tied to language, and analytical philosophy still carries a torch for speechless knowledge.

Behind this is no doubt the idea that there is a universal truth that lies behind deceptive language that one would like to find out despite everything. Nietzsche had already exposed the ridiculousness of the European delusion about truth. Far ahead of his time, he established that truth is always linguistically constituted. It is historical-cultural, not universal. With Wittgenstein, analytical philosophy also knows that a perfect language is a false

Thinking language 57

notion. However, instead of developing a fundamentally different approach to dealing with language and truth, this philosophy seems to draw the conclusion that it is no longer just the wrong way of speaking that is dangerous, but every form of speaking. So instead of thinking differently, it just expanded the combat zone.

Contrary to this tradition, which never managed to put its initial hostility to language behind it, language thinking lives an alternative: it sees no evil in the diversity and ambiguity of language and languages, but instead the richness and precisely the basis of our being.

Leibniz can perhaps be regarded as the founder of this completely different conception of language. He developed a teaching about the spirit which he called *pneumatics*, i.e. a teaching about breathing. His principle was *sympnoia panta*: everything breathes together. So in Leibniz we have a thinking of the connection between things. The spirit consists of a togetherness of all things, it is a breathing together. When mind is breath, the conclusion quickly drawn is that speech, which is sound and hearing and breath, is part of the overall sounding. Languages suddenly no longer appear as a hindrance to thinking and seeing, but are understood as part of the cosmic breath. In this way it becomes possible to understand the world with its diversity as harmony. As a result, diversity is no longer something terrible that needs to be fought but appears as a harmony of worlds in their diversity.

Accordingly, the study of languages – the study of all languages – pursues the goal of knowledge of the human mind. According to Leibniz, languages are the "best mirror of the human mind". He consequently develops a genuine way of thinking language: a form of thinking in which knowledge of the human mind grows from an understanding of the *wondrous multiplicity of its linguistic operations*.

In this spirit, the arbitrariness of meaning is no longer unbearable; on the contrary, it is wonderful and makes sense. We don't need any Adamic language in which word and thing agree. On the contrary, we need many different approaches to sound in unison. We are not in a state of complete arbitrariness since everything is related to everything else: everything responds and corresponds to everything else.

This notion of course stands in contrast to the prevailing western tradition, in which the world is to be grasped in a tangible way. It is about the deed, about an active influence on things. That is why the sense of sight is so crucial: it is a sense based on distance that enables a grasping understanding. For Leibniz's thinking, on the other hand, hearing is the fundamental sense. We cannot close our sense of hearing to the world. When we listen, we become one with what we hear, the sound fills us. We don't face the world, but rather the boundaries blur, the sound flows through the world and through us. The seer stands outside of what is seen, subject and object are separated; the listener resonates with the world, subject merges with object – indeed, the division into subject and object no longer makes sense.

That sounds very similar to many of today's esotericists. In fact, Leibniz has described his thinking as *acroamatic*, meaning accessible only to a small circle, only those who can gather around and listen to a speaker. To that extent, in Leibniz's time, acroamatics meant exactly what the term esoteric means in its literal sense: a teaching intended for those within a circle, for the small group of people who can be addressed directly.

Today, the term acroamatics is mainly used to mean a worldview that is not based on seeing, but on hearing. The ear, not the eye, is the most important organ for humanisation. The ear is crucial for language, without hearing the production of sounds would have no meaning, speech and language would not exist. Humans perceive themselves through their ears; as babies, they learn about themselves for the first time through their ears. A baby produces sounds, experiences itself as a doer, that is, as a poet, and these sounds then have noticeable and even life-saving consequences for it: it is heard and its needs are met. Its hearing gives it a sense of power through its voice. A baby also first perceives its environment through its hearing. In fact, we are already shaped in the womb by the sounds we hear. Our susceptibility to hearing is undeniable, and I am not referring here to the content of speech, but to sound and sounds. Music has a tremendous impact on our mood and we suffer from acoustic pollution and noise.

Herder spoke of man's obedience (*Hörigkeit*) to the world of the senses; hearing (*Hören*) is at the centre of his conception of language. For Herder, in contrast to Kant, there was no such thing as pure reason, only linguistic reason. In consequence, he introduced empiricism, specificity and historicity into abstract thinking.

In humans, language is not just sounds, it is concepts and thoughts. Thought and word are identical. Together they arise in the encounter with the world. So they are both internal cognitive events and world-related. This means that our thinking happens in interaction with the world. In other words, it is essentially dialogical.

Wilhelm von Humboldt also described language as "the formative organ of thought" – it is in language, then, that thought is created. Each thought in this "labour of the spirit" is unique to the speech in progress. Humboldt also emphasised the dialogical character of language. Not only does grammar presuppose the dialogical, since every I-saying is aimed at a You, but every utterance also requires the reaction of another. The linguistic-thinking synthesis is only complete when it returns to my ear via the speech of the other. We need confirmation via our own ears of the speech reflected in the other. This also includes the strengthening of the ear and acroamatics. Only together can the thought be completed.

This community ensures a certain universality, but above all it ensures that every linguistic utterance is historically unique, since everyone brings their own personal background to the table. One must therefore conclude that everyone has their own individual language, which is then also combined with other individual languages in the historical speech situation. This infinite and unavoidable variability of speaking moments forms the richness of our worldviews.

Truth is not the one truth but consists of all worldviews together. The more such views come together, the more comprehensive the picture of the world that emerges. An exhaustive knowledge of the world is in principle impossible, then, since every worldview always contains and adds something new. So instead of pursuing an idea of truth in which there is a certain fixed truth that is hiding somewhere and only needs to be discovered in order to be known and everything will be fine, we must accept that truth is always in flux and we are always working on it and are part of it. Otherwise we would have to assume that all the people who came before us were simply too stupid to find the truth or then kept it secret from everyone else. And sometime in the future, when we humans will finally be smart enough, the whole truth will be revealed, we will all be wise and there will be nothing more to do on earth. Unlikely.

And not at all desirable. A finite world is an abomination and the end of what is human.

No, our access to the world and to the truth is necessarily subjective. Due to the linguistic nature of our mental existence, we are inevitably in interaction with others, human life is determined by community. Truth is a collaborative effort. And that is in fact necessary for any development. Linguistic diversity is not a curse, but a blessing. Without it we would be idiots: if we consider the Greek root of this term: *το ιδιο* means one's own or the same – an idiot would therefore be someone who remains in themselves, who doesn't exchange with others.

Full speech is poetic – again in recourse to the Greek root of the term: ποιησις (*poiesis*) means to make or create. In speaking with one another, something that does not yet exist is created. This is how novelty comes into the world. Poetic speaking is therefore far from being just about the transfer of material, as current communication theories portray language, we are dealing in fact with a joint creative process. Language is ephemeral, it is not a product but an activity, as Humboldt put it. Language is both the individuality of each respective speech event as well as the totality of all speaking.

Instead of taking the πραξις (*praxis*), the mutual action of analytical philosophy, as a starting point, poetic thinking sets out from the ποιησις (*poiesis*) of semantic creativity. They are two different attitudes towards language. The poetic approach emphasises the process and creativity of speaking.

Every tiny individual difference in speech runs through the entire language. As such, it is an illusion to believe we can ever achieve full understanding. That really does require the miracle of Pentecost: the Holy Spirit has to arrive and take possession of those who are in conversation, then – at least – two people become one. That exists at least as a feeling, we call it love.

Apart from these moments of deep emotion, and probably even then, understanding is always at the same time non-understanding. Franz Werfel lamented this fact with the beautiful sentence "*Strangers we all are on earth*". But we should not lament this fact at all. Rather, it is absolutely necessary: without it, language would also be quite unnecessary, because it is always an attempt to overcome this fundamental difference. For this reason, as Jürgen Trabant puts it, language is "*a form of love*".

So it's a question of attitude, and a different attitude has extensive implications. If you are aware of this difference and strangeness, which not only exists between different language communities, but also within any given language community and between all individuals, and if you let it be and even welcome it, then you also adopt a different way of thinking. The truth is no longer a single "objective" matter, but it is the totality of all perspectives and can never be completed. That pulls the rug from under the feet of every claim to absoluteness, every totalitarian way of thinking.

Language thinking is anthropological thinking, since it answers the question of how humans create something new. This happens in language as the place of encounter between, on the one hand, the power of language with its conventions and frames of thought and, on the other, the dynamic power of the speaking human being, who, in every real speech event, goes beyond the linguistically given worldviews and pushes back the limits of the spirit. The more this happens, the more poetic the speaking becomes. All this makes it clear, too, that there is no special poetic language, only poetic speech. The poetic has nothing to do with the words used, nor is it determined by the chosen sentence structure. It's much more about linking the cognitive with the historical in the moment of speaking.

Descartes was still busy with the idea of two separate worlds. For him, one was the cognitive-mental one, which was completely independent of its medium, or, as he imagined it, thinking without a medium, i.e. without language. The other consisted of the material-communicative, in which the mental then found expression. Such an idea is opposed to language thinking. For language thinking, the mental is only formed in the process of language development, which is always in interaction with the outside world.

Humboldt used the expressions "language as sign" and "language as language" to describe the two different conceptions of language. When language is viewed as a sign, the creative process is no longer taken into account. The sign has already passed it by, it is no longer about the process of thinking, but only about knowing. Not that that is wrong – language is certainly also a sign. We just mustn't reduce it to that, because language is more than that. It must also be "language as language" so that it retains its vitality and its ability to develop and with it we humans likewise. Because the use of language as sign is so obvious and so necessary for everyday functioning, this aspect is dominant. Our culture tends to see only that dimension. But it is precisely against this dominance that true speech must be cultivated; a one-sided language culture leads to decline. Humans need *light and warmth* at the same time. Humboldt's motto points out that the rationality of the Enlightenment must always go hand in hand with the education of the heart.

Language thinking is an alternative to sign thinking. While we cannot escape sign thinking – as I said, we must also think in signs – we must understand that the sign is a historical concept, with its limitations and blind spots. Nor is our current western concept of rationality by any means the only conceivable one: we must expand it.

The sign consists of the designated (signified) and the designating (signifier). Although these are, as the founder of modern linguistics Ferdinand de Saussure said, as inseparable as two sides of a piece of paper, the concept of sign always involves the idea of something static and of a hierarchy: the signifier is secondary to the signified, which necessarily comes first. However, the value of any word is not exhausted by its semiotic dimension. It depends on its surroundings, its subjective associations and those that developed historically, on the respective language history and on the context of the utterance. None of this can be properly thought of from the sign. Language thinking is required, which involves *thinking the context*, i.e., to use Henri Meschonnic's term, the *continuous* of language (not thought of in terms of time, but as a unit of language expression). To think poetically is to think beyond the sign, to think this surplus. One can really only speak of language in terms of continuous speech, as Humboldt already stated: grammar and dictionary can barely be compared to language's "dead skeleton". Humboldt even thought that speech is not composed of its constitutive words but that the words only emerge from the speech as a whole. This language thinking really offers a different perspective on language: everything starts from language in its continuous. It considers language as alive, not as abstract composite parts. The continuous is what connects the words that, without context, would be meaningless.

Meschonnic developed the concept of *rhythm* to describe the organisation of this continuous (*le continu*): rhythm is the momentary unity in which the subject inscribes itself into discourse.

One should not, therefore, think of rhythm as a regular coming and going, or metre. Émile Benveniste showed that the original meaning of rhythm comes from ρειν (*rein*), meaning to flow, and was applied not to the waves of the sea but to the flow of a river. Consequently, rhythm denotes form in motion, devoid of organic consistency, an ever-changing form: improvised, momentary and mutable. From this idea of an unfixed, fleeting form, a fixed structural principle, metre, developed – but only since Plato. The concept of rhythm in language thinking, on the other hand, describes this form in motion.

Language has a dual function of meaning. First, it works in a semiotic way, that is, all linguistic units are considered as and in their unit, independent of all other units. On the other hand, it works semantically, that is, its meaning is understood holistically, with the sentence, or even better, the utterance, forming the smallest unit. The *sign* of semiotics is *recognised*, the *discourse* (as Benveniste called this unit of utterance) of semantics is *understood*. An anecdote about the theatre director Stanislavski serves to clarify the difference. He had an actor pronounce the words *sevodnja večerom* (tonight) in forty different ways, each time conveying a different meaning, such as surprise, anticipation, determination. Recognising words is simply not enough to understand their meaning. One and the same word can mean all sorts of things.

While the sign divides language into disconnected elements, discourse looks at the continuum, the context. Of course, working with a small unit is more practical for analysis, but this prevents thinking the whole language. It's also no coincidence that most linguists don't work with poetry, because sign thinking fails when doing so. Meaning is always dependent on the continuous. The sign, however, does not make any sense; sense only grows out of the discourse as a whole, in what is concretely and coherently spoken in its particular historical circumstances.

In discourse, the speaking person manifests herself as a subject. Every time one says I, subjectivity takes place, and each time a new instance of it – the subjectivity of the speaker cannot be permanently fixed, it is unique every time. Accordingly, language is always that of the person speaking, subject to the condition of intersubjectivity. One becomes a subject in the practice of language. However, since the I-saying always takes place in relation to a you, there must be another subject when speaking, because it is only together that an I and a you can really speak. Being a subject is always constituted in such speaking. Meschonnic puts it this way: "Subject is through whom another is subject." Accordingly, speaking fully means being subjects for one another. Such language thinking obviously has ethical consequences. People are in a mutual relationship here. I will return to this crucial dialogic moment of speaking and being a subject in the next chapter.

It is only by way of language that everything that is given becomes determinable for humans. It all becomes real and world. "The thing" only becomes available when it becomes language. One can therefore say that only language produces human reality. And this human reality is necessarily subjective. People must therefore cultivate such subjective speech. That is how they establish a connection to the truth, expand the boundaries of the world and, crucially, keep the human alive.

Poetic thinking involves these processes. Language thinking is naturally required if one wants to think the poetic aspect of literature. But what is crucial about it can be transferred to art in general. Art does not have to fulfil any objective truth conditions. Because of this "dishonesty", it is often condemned by social utopias, from Plato to the French Revolution. The totalitarianisms of the twentieth century then largely take it into their service, which means it loses its essential independence and can no longer genuinely be art.

Art has survived every persecution; it seems to represent a necessity. Nonetheless, it will never be able to take a central place in society, it is naturally on the fringes and cannot be integrated into the practical context of society as that would destroy its freedom from the latter's criteria. It is precisely in this marginal position that its function lies. It has a utopian quality, and society needs that to develop new ways of life, new ways of acting and thinking. The faster the living conditions in society change, the more we need this laboratory of the mind and the senses to develop ways of dealing with the new.

It is necessary to include once more the concept of attitude, because that makes all the difference: in the poetic, the practical context of action is not central as it is in sign thinking, but rather the contemplation and perception of the phenomenon as such. If one now starts from the abundance of perceptual possibilities and from the full range of linguistic possibilities, then art or poetic speech is by no means a special form of objective sign language as it is usually portrayed, but quite the contrary, the poetic is full speaking, while the regular speaking of language as a sign represents a narrowing and reduction of language. Poetic speaking is therefore not pruned speaking. All encrustations and automatisms make the poetic impossible, they must be broken open for perception to occur.

Art can of course give birth to little monsters as well, but they tend to lack the teeth to really wreak havoc. Art is a social laboratory in which new things are played through relatively safely and the future is designed. Therefore, art is vital to any society and must be protected and promoted. Society renews itself here and keeps fit for new requirements. Also, social life would be impoverished without it. In art, the key concepts of relationships in human life are negotiated and shaped. If people don't want to be reduced to vegetating and if they don't want to fail in the face of new demands from a changing environment, society must always develop alternative structures of thought and action. Linguistic-mental diversity is the basis for all alternative thinking. It is the only way to overcome problems, a condition for survival. In this sense, poetry, understood as full poetic speaking, is indeed the distinction of the species. The human cannot be separated from the poetic. The poetic, as Humboldt put it, is "a glimmering spark in animal torpor".

Language in the full sense is precisely a poetic excess of being human, in which this being is first constituted. It is a gleaming spark, humanity is potentialistic, as I have already called it: it appears in propitious moments, in *kairos*. In these moments we go beyond social functioning, with this surplus we achieve wholeness.

So in speaking and thinking there is a constant battle between the rule-bound and predetermined character of language on the one hand and the freedom of speaking on the other. This battle is waged most intensely in literature. It exists everywhere, but here it is programmatic, so to speak. It's here that the labour of the spirit takes place. The poetic is therefore not synonymous with a classical notion of beauty but is precisely this excess of human creativity, which is inexplicable, and it is in this that the anthropological distinction lies. The essence of language consists precisely in its going-beyond-functioning. The poetic is ultimately language itself, in which human beings come into their own.

In interaction with other people, we form our chaotic sensual experiences of the world into language, we put them into words and only in this way do those experiences become comprehensible to us. In this way, we give ourselves our own world made of language. We become ourselves in language. The essence of language is the excess of the poetic. Literature is the place where this is played out in the most pronounced way. Within literature, this happens most powerfully in the poem. In poetic speaking, then, we have the most intense humanity, not because of emotionality and expressiveness, but because of the "labour of the spirit" (Humboldt), which is language and which takes place most urgently in such speaking.

In art, semantics is crucial; semiotics, of course, also exists but does not touch the essence of art. Its analytical thinking can only ever think aspects of the artwork, not art. The specific meaning of the work of art lies only in its unity. To have an art experience requires a shift in attention. The sign cannot think the specificity of the work of art, it has no poetic thinking.

Poetic thinking wants to create opportunities to think the phenomenon of art, the poetic. Otherwise our thinking is incomplete and our view of life is limited. In order to process the world mentally, to labour it with one's spirit, we must put it into words: language is fundamental to our awareness of the world. Language theory is crucial for every science of meaning – and for our relationship with the world.

Our knowledge landscape harbours its own form of ignorance, it has blind spots that the system simply cannot be aware of. Anything outside sign logic can be brushed aside as irrational. That's a pity because it blocks crucial life contexts.

We must develop ways of thinking the process of being. The poetic is not a product, it is the activity itself – Humboldt established this for language thinking: language is not *ergon* (product), but *energeia* (activity). In this process, a transformation takes place. The poetic as transformation exerts an effect by altering man's relationship with the world. So there is an interrelationship between the poetic and life. Form of language and form of life are mutually dependent. The poetic invents the subject, so to speak; it is a way of thinking in which a transformation of the subject occurs. Since our world is largely constituted by our relationship with it, transforming our relationship with the world also changes our world.

When poetic thinking speaks of the subject, it is not really about the person, but about the process of subjectivation, about the activity itself. It is therefore a matter of a radically historical conception of the subject. The subject exists only in the mode of the present, always, and is particular in every moment. Therefore, it cannot be imposed on anything or anyone. It cannot be viewed in the past and is unpredictable for the future.

In language thinking, then, language is conceived of in terms of the subjectification of language when speaking. It thereby assumes historicity rather than structure. In speaking, language and the subject constantly begin anew. The poetic thus shows the failure of the sign with its thinking of form and content, of sound and meaning. Signs can be exchanged; the poetic cannot be expressed in any other way. In a different form it is no longer the same. The poetic is more than signs. Poetic thinking points to the weakness of the existing sign thinking and develops a different thinking. It's a matter of the conception of the self.

Thinking the context also gives rise to the possibility of thinking presence. Presence cannot be understood and mastered – and we have already established that this is a good thing. We do not need definitive analyses and conclusions in this regard. But the existence of presence must be brought to our awareness and cultivated, for it is life itself. Poetic thinking is about developing concepts with which to approach art and literature. The crucial point about the present is its openness and its fluctuation, its never definitive but living nature, which is denied by our usual form of knowledge. Poetic thinking constantly withdraws from every system of thought and offers a retreat from all systems. That's why poetic thinking is such a challenge for us. In a certain sense, poetic thinking cannot succeed at all in the long term, but that is also inherent in its task from the outset. If it succeeded, in our usual sense of scientific knowledge, it would be a failure. It's a paradox. However, we would lose a truly essential dimension of human life if we gave up this paradoxical task – which, in my view, is impossible anyway. Attempts to think art and literature are paramount for a reflection and awareness of ourselves.

The poetic affects everyone, their subjectivity and the emergence of the new in the world – it is essential for culture in its entirety. Its historicity shows the infinity of being, contrary to any totalitarian thinking. It creates a connection to our own ignorance, expanding the limits of our mind and thus widening the limits of our spirit and broadening our horizons time and again. It wants to think all aspects of life and consequently sees itself as a greater realism. When poetic thinking seeks to think the mystery of human existence and cultivate it, that is by no means an escape from life, but rather a grounding of thinking.

10 Dialogical thinking

Dialogics is similarly about the concrete historical encounter as the basis of thinking and our idea of being. Dialogical thinking is one of the cornerstones of poetic thinking alongside language thinking. When people talk about "dialogue" today, they usually mean the banal fact that dialogue is necessary for society. "Willingness to engage in dialogue", "to conduct a dialogue", those are everyday terms used to express willingness to compromise and show respect. They are nice things, but they stand for a very simple concept of communication and so have little to do with dialogical thinking.

Dialogical thinking includes an ontological dimension: although it is of course based on concrete relationships between people, it is about the whole: about being. In the dialogical mode of being, the world is perceived in the sense of poetic thinking, so there is a transformation of feeling, thinking, perception in the interaction of the form of language and the form of life.

There has certainly always been a knowledge of the conditionality of being through mutual relationship, which is probably a significant part of what used to be called wisdom – a term that is now out of fashion. Yet it is certainly no coincidence that dialogical thought received increased attention and systematic treatment precisely at the time of the Enlightenment. With the Enlightenment, people became detached from their contexts, on the one hand due to the change in the economic system, but on the other due to the spread of analytical thinking, in which the focus was on individual components instead of the big picture. Of course, this increased reflection has also led to higher consciousness, including self-awareness. This in turn led to a stronger subject-object separation and a greater distance between the observer and the observed. So it is in contrast to these tendencies that an awareness of the inseparable connection between I and you also took place, as a counter-movement to the I-thinking of the conscious Cartesian subject.

The dialogical thinking that developed in the eighteenth century criticised the limited conception of the subject, in which thinking was based only on the ego. The self-aware, unified and controlled subject ought also to rule the world, that was the programme of the general western tradition of thought. On the other hand, thinkers like Hamann, Herder and Jacobi brought the relationship between I and you to the fore. Jacobi was then able to come up with the following: "Without a you, the I is impossible."

In 1827, Humboldt provided the language-theoretical basis for this way of thinking by emphasising the unchangeable dualism in language. Another person is not only indispensable for mental and emotional needs, no, the person needs a "you" corresponding to the "I" "also just for the sake of his own thinking". An extra I is the condition for every conceptual formation. For thinking to occur, two thinking forces are necessary, one person alone is unable to do it. Of course, this shouldn't be taken too simplistically. It goes without saying that you can also sit alone in your little room and think. Most thought products come from lonely thinking and writing. This lonely thinking and pondering is, however, always done in exchange with other thinkers. Whether they are physically present or not, they are necessarily there in spirit. Linguistically speaking, the "I" is always opposed to the "you" in the sphere of joint action. The he/she/it, on the other hand, is always just a not-I and a not-you, the he/she/it does not stand for themselves, but represents something. By contrast, we can identify what is decisive about the you as follows: it does not stand for an object, does not represent anything, but is part of a shared sphere.

In 1843, Ludwig Feuerbach formulated his *Philosophy of the Future*: "The essence of man is contained only in the unity of man with man." Being human can only be thought of as a dialogue. For the I, consciousness of the world is mediated only through a consciousness of the You. Man alone is nothing, he can only come into existence through community. This philosophy of the future then disappeared for a long time and even if the idea has become more widespread in the meantime, it has still not been thoroughly integrated by philosophy to this day, so it remains a *philosophy of the future*.

It was only with the expression and catalyst of the crisis in the west, the First World War, that this dialogical idea could begin to develop again. Hermann Cohen, Franz Rosenzweig, Martin Buber, Ferdinand Ebner, Eugen Rosenstock and many more in the first fifteen years after the war – thinkers from diverse backgrounds, though largely in the Jewish tradition – emphasised the importance of the you for human life. With National Socialism, however, this dialogical thinking was cut short again and has since been on the sidelines of the history of philosophy. As I said, today's fashionable term "dialogic" lags far behind the meaning of *New Thinking*, as Rosenzweig called it. However, especially in the twenty-first century, the need to become aware of our need for others is pressing. We have to give the you, the stranger and the Other a bigger place if we want to respect everyone's dignity in a globalised world and create a functioning community. There have always been isolated publications on dialogics, and the prestigious publisher Karl Alber's series *Dia-Logik*, in existence since 2011, is a sign that it has not been forgotten but on the contrary continues to have the power to stimulate.

Language is also an essential element in the dialogical, especially with Ebner and Rosenzweig. Ebner describes language as something "utterly transcendent". However, in contrast to poetic thinking, Ebner and Rosenzweig share the theological dimension: language is ultimately the expression of, and the connection to, God, the word of God is final. Nonetheless, there are significant parallels. Ebner considers dialogical thought to be life itself. The "you" is given to humans in language, through the word. So the word creates the human being, in the current spoken exchange, between "I" and "you".

Rosenzweig regards language as subjectivity and objectivity at the same time; perception of the world is shaped by language, which in turn is shaped by humans. Humans themselves are language, as such they are the bridge between one human and another, between humans and society, and between humans and the world. It is impossible to go too far in thinking of language and human beings as identical, Bruno Liebrucks said, following Humboldt. Our selfhood and self-confidence as human beings are possible only through language.

In Rosenzweig, too, we find the idea of direct life or being. He criticises the history of philosophy for starting from the given and thus ignoring the essential. The special thing is the gift, that which is always new. This is clearly a thinking of the event; it is once again about presence. Life and thinking are in tension with each other. Rosenzweig's *The New Thinking* is a personal standpoint philosophy against "the professional impersonality of philosophers". That is why he wants to break open philosophy. He wants to achieve this by introducing the concept of revelation. His approach is theological.

In contrast to philosophical thinking, which he describes as timeless and alone, i.e. as standing outside of the concrete historical situation, his language thinking is conversation. This means that you never know in advance what will happen. You don't know what the other will say, nor what you yourself will say. It is an eventful encounter with an open ending. Something happens, together with a concrete, existing other. Rosenzweig's criticism of the I-philosophy of "idealism", as he calls it, is a declaration of war on the history of philosophy, which in consequence punishes him with disregard.

Dialogical thinking assumes that all being is already being-with. The history of philosophy has difficulties thinking in terms of this dialogical, linguistic composition of our world experience. There are, however, always voices in philosophy that address it. Jean-Luc Nancy pointed out in the early 1990s that co-existence precedes existence and that each I emerges from a we, just as each we in turn forms a new singularity. So in our singularity we are always founded in the plural. Shortly thereafter, Peter Sloterdijk began his sphere work, in which the *bubble* represents the original sphere. Spheres are to be thought of as spaces that people create in order to produce their own possibilities of being. The bubble is one such space for two. Every person is originally part of such a bubble or a two-person relationship, only later does this dual unit get lost with the incorporation of the original bubble into *foam*, i.e. into a huge accumulation and clustering of such bubbles. But even if this foam obscures the view of the dual bubble, the idea of an individual's private sphere is a fiction, because the bubble can never be completely extinguished.

Sloterdijk points to the tremendous importance of the placenta in many cultures throughout world history, in which it was revered as a nourishing shadow and anonymous sibling. It was regarded as a remedy, revered, consumed, carried around constantly – in almost all older cultures birth and afterbirth were regarded as corresponding and belonging to each other. It wasn't until the eighteenth century that the Enlightenment made the placenta a disgusting, discarded thing and trained people to feel revulsion, so that today it is treated as waste. This rejection of the placenta corresponds to a disregard for our dyadic constitution as humans.

This narrowing of the concept of reason and the suppression of a more embodied thinking and the fundamental duality of the human leads to dangerous replacement manoeuvres: modern humans are detached from the co-space of the duality bubble and instead either go on a manic hunt for substitute collectives, often with their "people", which in turn often leads to the exclusion of others, or they succumb to loneliness, which easily degenerates into depression unless they successfully practise techniques of solitude. The recent cultivation of alternative approaches to clinical positivism gives grounds for hope, for instance a culture of midwives who ritualise the cutting of the umbilical cord: after all, the umbilicus is the monument to a human duality that has become unthinkable.

The human being is therefore never the centre, but always to be considered within a human field. In this respect, environment (around-world is the literal version of the German term, "Umwelt") is already a misleading term – we would have to speak of *in-world* or *with-world*, in which resonances are decisive. There are no individuals whatsoever, all people as poles of bubbles are always "dividuals". The idea of the individual is the result of the repression of the basic pair structure. If we turn our attention to this largely forgotten basic relationship of being human, current notions of human living conditions appear banal and limited.

Such knowledge about human relations exists in the most diverse areas of society, but it is denied in the business world and unfortunately also to a great extent in academia. Thinking poetically also means eliminating this split in the world of knowledge.

Human life is therefore always primarily being-with, it is dialogical, that is, ambi-guous. Philosophy and the sciences, however, strive for unambiguousness – this can probably not be achieved in the human sciences, which are sciences of meaning.

In my reflections on language thinking, I referred to the role of *hearing*. Acroamatics emphasises that hearing precedes speaking. It is not for nothing that thinkers like Jacobi and Schopenhauer pointed out that reason (*Vernunft*) comes from hearing (*Vernehmen*). That too is confirmed and proven by dialogics.

According to Rosenzweig's language thinking, people always name things when speaking, but the things carry with them all previous names along with the historical circumstances of all those names. This is how the human cohesion is created. Humans never exist in general, but only as concrete people. Humanity is always absent, only the people are always present, you and I. But the language in its presence and its tradition, in the confrontation of the word with its entire history and what is currently being said, connects humanity and things. Here we come across the metaphor of the world as text, as a large fabric – text in fact means fabric – in which we inscribe ourselves at every moment. This is an infinite process, with no origin or end.

That is the principle of Talmud reading in the Jewish tradition. Since only the consonants are written in Hebrew, the idea of reading is a much more active one than in the Christian tradition. Readers virtually write along with the text in their update since they must fill in so many blanks. And so an understanding of the text developed that is not fixed, but processual and infinite. All speech is like a thread in this fabric. We can never measure the fabric as a whole, but every time we speak we are woven into the whole – we are connected with humanity.

Accordingly, the idea of the true essence of things is absurd: the truth only ever appears on a case-by-case basis, but it must prove itself against the you. Rosenzweig speaks of the "proof of truth" that takes place dialogically, in the dialogically spoken word. Thinking is thus historicised by linking it back to dialogics – it is always about the concrete situation between concrete people. The logic of pure thinking does not exist in life. In reality, we can only ever experience the world in the other, in the you of the other who actually encounters us.

Turning to Martin Buber, who formulated the dialogical principle most impressively, we find that the basis for his thinking lies in Eastern Jewish Hasidism. This faith community made overcoming the distance between the sacred and the profane the core of its life practice: humans must reach God through their everyday actions. Behind this is the conviction that God needs man in order to come into the world. It is therefore the responsibility of humans to make the world divine and to ensure God's existence on earth.

To that end, we, the humans, must relate to people and things. The crisis of western man, which has preoccupied us since the dawn of modernity, is a crisis in our relationship with the world around us, the world-with-us. It is a crisis of the *in-between*. Dialogical thinking is a thinking of the in-between – and thus its cultivation. This term will become clearer on the following pages. The interpersonal, for instance, is the participation of the other person in one's own being.

Being itself appears as a "whirlwind of events", as Buber calls it – we are exposed to it and cannot control it. We can protect ourselves against it by blocking ourselves from being and closing ourselves off from it or by putting on armour. But we can also expose ourselves to it and enter into being, surrender ourselves to the whirlwind. In that case reality is transcended into actuality. So I am drawing a distinction between *reality*, that is, the given, and *actuality*, momentary life integrated into the world, in which the given appears as a gift. In such moments of actuality humans *actualise* the world. It is only in actualising that they themselves become actual.

Buber claimed the existence of two basic words: on the one hand there is the I-You and on the other hand the I-It. Depending on which I you speak, you adopt a different basic attitude. You always speak the I-You with your whole being, the I-It by contrast never. We are generally in an I-It relationship with the world, this is our everyday experience. In experiencing, we separate our subject-being from the objects, we are a self-being that distinguishes itself from other self-beings. That is not inherently bad, it is in fact necessary to function in society and to organise one's life. However, this I-It relationship must not predominate, otherwise it suppresses actualisation because it keeps people in an attitude that does not allow it.

For actualisation to occur, we must be in the I-You relationship. In this form of being we are no longer separated from the world, our subjectivity is no longer opposed to objects, but the relationality itself makes up our subjectivity. So there is no longer a subject-object separation, we are rather in a subject-subject relationship. Only then are we really a *person*. In the I-You both poles of the relationship are framed in reciprocity, they are no longer objects. Since we no longer look at the other from the outside, we know everything and nothing about them, just as we know that about ourselves. Incidentally, we can also come to things in an I-You relationship, but then reciprocity is not fully developed – for that another person is needed.

Person and own-being are the two modes of being of the human – which I is spoken, whether we are in I-You or I-It mode, is the basic distinguishing feature. Even if the true *encounter* is sent "by grace", a certain attitude is helpful to get into the I-You relationship. As I said, you can armour yourself or let things happen. A striving for relationality promotes the occurrence of the I-You.

This I-You is obviously a moment of presence; it is pure presence. That's why it cannot be located in the dimensions of time and space. It is lost whenever it is to be mapped. As soon as you refer to it, it is no longer there. This is the phenomenon of presence. In this context, Jacques Derrida spoke of "différance": the unavoidable displacement in relation to the event leads to an irresolvable difference between event and representation. The events themselves tear "dangerously to the extremes", as Buber puts it, precisely because the verifiable It-world breaks up and collapses. It's uncanny, because the tried and tested structures have fallen away – you're out in the open.

The presence of the You on a permanent basis is unbearable. To that extent it must always become an object, it must become It. We can only endure being as the here and now that has been detached from time – it cannot be lived in the long term. Also, our experience can only enter our cognition as It: it must become an object in order to be an object of knowledge. The I-It is the common world, the I-You seldom breaks open or breaks in.

But these You-moments are indispensable, they make up what it means to be human. The I-You belongs to the whole human being, only in it does the human being find the purpose of its being. The I-It, however, always proliferates. It is necessary, but equally dangerous when it overruns us and thus de-actualises us, when it reigns alone without the I-You. In saying that, I am by no means denying what is conceptually comprehensible; the I-You is merely intended to show the existence of something that goes beyond. This going beyond is precisely the primary thing, it is the "cradle of actual life". Only the I-You adds a dimension to human life that makes it human – it is the surplus that we have also highlighted as an essential part of language. The I-It cannot grasp this dimension, it does not perceive it and thus blocks its own perception of the You.

The parallel between I-You and I-It on the one hand and language thinking and sign thinking on the other is striking. A parallel can also be drawn with Nietzsche's Dionysian and Apollonian. The Dionysian is the intoxicating force that breaks open the structures and represents pure life, whereas the Apollonian derives a form from this event. So they are complementary parts; both are necessary for human life.

The return to the origin of life must be accomplished time and again. The origin must, however, not be understood as a point in time in the past, rather the origin is what takes place over and over in the I-You moments. Being human begins in every moment. Dialogical thinking is a thinking of presence, out of immanence. So with the concept of the in-between we return to the concept of immanent transcendence. Like language and spirit, poetic thinking is not in the I, but in-between I and You.

Essential humanity takes place in the dialogically spanned in-between. Hölderlin wrote "since we have been a conversation and can hear from one another": we humans *are* conversation, conversation of course here in the dialogically charged sense, not just small talk. In entering the space of conversation, in the in-between, we experience our humanity. The poetic is the in-between that has taken shape. That's why it touches us. We can only perceive it by re-entering this I-You ourselves.

Dialogical thinking does not answer the anthropological question by referring to a group of living beings, but instead with a particular way of being. The basic characteristics of human beings are not located in the being-for-oneself of the human being, they are only found in the categories of being human with human beings – in the interpersonal relationship. The decisive factor here is the non-object-being, the subject-subject relationship of I-You. "Humanity and mankind become actual encounters", says Buber. Humans are spirit, nature and community.

Anthropological reflection comes only when you lose yourself. As long as you "have" yourself as an object, you only experience people as objects. They don't yet have wholeness, that only comes with being. This poses a problem because it is not detectable. The I-You does not lead to an objectively valid knowledge of being, but it can offer genuine contact with the other. Reflection (Besinnung) means becoming senses (Sinne), being embodied and perceiving – it is the opposite of contemplation, which always takes place at a remove in time.

The human is therefore the being in whose currently present being-as-two the encounter between I and You is realised. Thus, the I-You has a special dimension, it spans its own space of being, the *in-between*, for these fleeting events that create the basis for our existence. With the in-between, then, we are dealing neither with the traditional subject nor with the object, it lies beyond the subjective and this side of the objective. Henri Meschonnic defines the subject of the poem as being a subject through whom another is a subject. It is precisely this idea that can be found in language thinking and dialogical thinking and that is also at the core of poetic thinking. We only really are when we are in this sphere of the in-between.

The dialogical is also a potentialist anthropology: the in-between is suddenly actualised but underlies everything. It is nothing fixed or secured. The dialogical can indeed be promoted by an attitude, but if and when it will happen cannot be known. It cannot be achieved through rules and regulations. Anyone can experience it if they surrender to it instead of withholding. Its potential is open to all human beings, and only human beings. This makes it the essence of humanity. Humans become human through a surplus for which only they have the potential.

The representation of the surplus is a problem. It belongs in the realm of art. The in-between is not directly translatable, it lives only in the moment and is fleeting. It is not possible to make a definite statement about presence, but we can, as Buber puts it, cultivate the "certainty of encountering what remains veiled". Its existence must be recognised by philosophy, even if it is arguably outside philosophical categories and beyond its traditional boundaries. My reflections on poetic thinking and Buber's writings on dialogics are also a concession to the It; the unique is transformed into the general. But that's not a problem, it's about the mediation between I-You and I-It.

Poetic thinking offers a coherent context yet not a logical system – that would be impossible. It is not a teaching, but rather a demonstration of actuality that is otherwise not seen enough. It takes on the bloated hubris of the I-It, which can be put back in its place by the I-You at any moment, since humankind begins at any moment, with every I-You. On the other hand, the poetic is powerless in direct conflict with power, it can never fight an opponent, but it can overpower anyone from within. Much would be gained if our society feared this form of being overwhelmed less and armed itself less against it.

To do this, we must first accept a more comprehensive concept of reason. We should redefine reason as the ability to see and understand what is. The poetic exists, no doubt. When the early Wittgenstein asserted the existence of the unspeakable, which he also called the mystical, but then rejected any talk about it for philosophy, analytical philosophy renounced thinking about essential aspects of human existence. A mode of reason that has no access to the poetic is in bad shape. Starting from the concrete dialogical situation, on the other hand, an immanent transcendence can be reached.

Poetic thinking cannot solve the problem of becoming conscious of being, nor does it intend to, but it can include it and allow this surplus to exist rather than ignore it. That does not establish a universally valid ethical system, which in any case is not possible. It merely describes an attitude from which much can follow.

11 The meaning and purpose of poetic thinking

While meaning and purpose may at times coincide, they are two very different things. Purpose stems from functional thinking: there are clear premises about what is to be achieved, and one acts accordingly. Meaning, on the other hand, is something that always arises from a certain action, it cannot be predetermined. However, meaning of course also has a purpose, and a very important one at that. Humans cannot do without meaning. It is absolutely necessary so that we do not despair of our existence. We are doomed to create meaning over and over again so as not to atrophy and perish. Giving meaning is therefore also a purpose in life.

That is why poetic thinking is so indispensable for human life. As I have explained, language is ambiguous precisely because the speakers speak in their personality, that is, in their uniqueness and diversity – qualities that are necessary for lively speech, for presence and for the acceptance of the other. This ambiguity, uniqueness and diversity must be integrated into thinking: they must be made thinkable, or thinking must at least be done in such a way that they are not crushed. We must tolerate what is alien in our thinking, including what is alien in ourselves. Paradoxically, such an acknowledgement of the alien is at the same time the only possible way of overcoming the feeling of alienation, since recognised alienness is no longer perceived as alienating but is part of our being.

Speaking is therefore always speaking-nonetheless, despite the impossibility of complete agreement. It involves making an effort with what is foreign and with that effort foreignness can to a certain extent be overcome. That is why Jürgen Trabant can also describe speaking as *a form of love*.

In such loving speaking, something new is made together each and every time. Poetic thinking includes this specific condition, it knows about foreignness since it is a mode of thinking of and in language. The poetic is always something that is not yet known, it has to come to you. Anything expected, no matter how gratifying, cannot be poetic. This does not mean, however, that the poetic must be new in the sense of the avant-garde. It is not a question of something materially new, but of a new experience. That is, it results from the in-between that occurs in each case, in the interplay of man and world. The essence of language is not the communication of something already thought but the inexplicable excess. It is the process of becoming meaningful, the emergence of something new.

Poetic thinking is therefore language thinking that does not yet know what there is to communicate. It is letting language come, listening to something that is not yet there. Of course, something that can be grasped can also come up for discussion. Above all, however, it is about the very existence of what does not yet have a form. In this sense, the poetic is pure *poiesis*, pure creation of something new. Remembering that there is such a thing is the essential part of the poetic, its importance is not to be underestimated. Poetic thinking is a concession to that which is open and does not yet exist, but which as such may lay claim to meaning and space in the world. It keeps the possibility of the new open.

This is also the importance and one of the main tasks of today's poetry. It must show that the poetic exists. If art gives up this task, who or what should take it over? And when it is no longer given any place in the world, this world is lost, since it can only revolve around itself. A swindle.

The poetic must provide a counterpoint to the supposed domination of the world through knowledge, feasibility and calculability. It refers to the mysteriousness of being, which leads to a form of attention that allows an I-You relationship and thus an attitude to life and the world that amazes. In this amazement, the distance inherent in sign thinking and subject-object-thinking is eliminated. It is precisely the poem that is capable of portraying this detachment from everything applicable. This denial of what is functional, practical and expedient is part of poetic thinking. It is a focus on being and accordingly the opposite of entertainment, consumption and excitement. It precisely doesn't want to be pulled out of itself – *excited* – but to go into itself, as a movement of concentration. Becoming aware instead of succumbing to speed. But such concentration is never possible on its own, something is always added to this movement. That is due to our basic dialogical condition: we are not individuals but dividuals. And as such we are receptive to the world; we are all ears. Poetically thinking, we *resonate*: we vibrate in the sound space of the world.

If languages are the *cathedrals of thought*, as Jürgen Trabant says, then poetic thinking is a form of devotion: the structure that has grown out of the common culture, together with the time spent in it, in other words, the individually formative animating of a given framework, renders service to culture and to life. This points to the need for language cultivation in everyday conversation. We must develop and cultivate forms of conscious linguistic expression of complex life so as not to become spiritually impoverished.

If that is to be achieved, we must first of all raise awareness of the importance of language thinking. This is a major challenge for educational policy. Schools must promote language thinking from an early age. They must practise real *philology* in a well-developed English class; in other words, cultivate the love of language. So instead of asking students when dealing with literature to pursue the question of what the author wants to say, they themselves must begin a conversation with the language and the literature. They must formulate in a literary way for themselves and so experience what effect the process of bringing forth language has on thinking. Such an approach to linguistic creativity allows knowledge to be gained where analytical language, which considers itself neutral, reaches its limits, and that triggers further thought processes. This formation of language awareness automatically promotes the characteristics decisive for today's society, namely cooperation, participation and creativity.

This is an educational requirement that must begin at a young age but must also be continued in adult education. Especially in our time, education is becoming enormously important, since an ever-growing proportion of the population is unemployed and therefore left to its own devices. Both the unemployed and the elderly should not be limited to television or internet clips, which are usually of very poor quality, in their dealings with the world. They must develop options for dealing with their own personal encounter with self and world. Poetic thinking can do much here in the form of creative writing seminars in which language thinking is encouraged. Such further training should obviously also be rolled out to managers and business elites to incorporate dialogical dimensions and creativity into business processes. Dealing with aphorisms and poems can also show how such open structures often achieve more in concrete human interaction than overly fixed conventional rules of conduct. Vast fields lie fallow here for a new legitimation of the humanities and the university.

In addition to such basic language and thinking lessons in the national language – and this obviously underlines the absolute priority for language support for immigrants – foreign language teaching must also be promoted. And it's not just a question of international communication skills, which should of course be encouraged, but also of an in-depth experience of another culture. Only through such an experience of a foreign culture can an awareness of one's own culture be achieved at the same time as its relativisation. The ERASMUS programme, in which students study abroad for one or two semesters, is an important step in this direction and should be further expanded. A new Europe is genuinely being created here, with a generation that has largely experienced diversity as an opportunity and an enrichment of life.

Poetic thinking, by its very nature, is never achieved in the sense that one has learned it and then is capable of it and does it. It is something that must be created anew in every moment, the constant labour of the spirit. In this respect, it is also quite unnecessary to despair of it and to tell yourself that you just can't get it right. We don't always think poetically, that wouldn't work either. Most of the time we think in terms of concrete contexts of action in which we must function. Poetic thinking, however, is a corrective that reminds us again and again that we must not lose sight of our humanity beyond this functioning.

It is a toe-hold for a reaction to the crisis of western thinking, which was the starting point of these considerations. Sign thinking and subject-object-thinking, the foundations of both the success and the crisis of the west, are attitudes to reality which, by distancing, on the one hand enable control, and on the other prevent our being in agreement with ourselves. As long as we understand reason as nothing more than an instrument for self- and world-control, there is an unbridgeable difference between the world and this *ratio* understood as our being. Presence becomes impossible and, as a result, also transcendence and the openness of being. We live in the idea of a finite world. That is good for purpose-oriented thinking. For meaning, however, which needs openness, it is fatal.

In a finite world there is also a tendency towards biopolitics of the body. If humans are considered only from the point of view of purpose-oriented efficiency, they are little more than biomass: that entails the danger of totalitarianism. As soon as their right to exist is measured by their functional value in power strategies, they are merely a factor independent of their personality.

Instead, to think the human as poetic thinking does, we must always start from the encounter. In the name of this kind of meaning, nothing can be sacrificed at all, since this in-between can only ever represent a beginning, never an end.

There is no such thing as being an abstract human being, nor are there any abstract basic conditions of being human. Humans are never possible other than in social spheres. The individual is a dividuum, for a consciousness of the I, the You is required. This is the opposite of the crowd. In the crowd, individuals come out of themselves and become one with it, but they also lose themselves. Moreover, mass bonding always works against others and the particular has no place in it. In the dialogical, on the other hand, it is always the relationship that counts in its particularity. That is why the crowd is never human, whereas human beings become human at the very moment when they make another human, in this indissoluble duality, independent of group affiliation or other desires.

This in no way precludes a sense of connection with the community, on the contrary. When the dialogical is recognised as the basis of our actions, our varied connection with the world moves into the centre of our being. We are then in touch with our world. Accordingly, all our activities can no longer be assigned to a concrete purpose but serve the purpose of life. Our work, for example, would no longer be understood merely as gainful employment, it would then also be the integration of our abilities and skills into the greater whole.

In poetic thinking there is therefore a *potentialist anthropology*: humans are not already and always human, they only become so in the moment of a truly human I-You relationship. These moments are open to everyone as a potential that can be hindered or promoted through socialisation and attitude, but which is never guaranteed and always possible. In this respect, nobody is more or less human, everyone possesses this potential at every moment. The criterion of the human is a *possibility*. Humanity is not understood here as a biological species, but as a claim on the individual.

In today's bioethics debates, on the other hand, the focus is increasingly on the rights of the community, to which individual rights must take second place. Especially in recent years, the approach has shifted: instead of protecting human dignity as the dignity of the individual, it is about an abstract human being who represents a group of people. This is evident in a renewed acceptance of the torture discourse, particularly in the wake of US practices at Abu Ghraib, in which individual human dignity was sacrificed for the protection of the community. The COVID-19 mandatory vaccination debate is another case in point. But it also makes itself felt in comparatively harmless measures that affect the entire population even more, for example, in the surveillance of public space, where the protection of privacy takes a back seat to the supposed fight against crime. Evidently, this is already following us far beyond the public sphere into our barely existing private sphere, for example by means of the verifiability of our movements and needs through mobile phones and the internet, or through big data and the creation of personality profiles by evaluating our consumer behaviour.

Precision has a high value in our society, the sciences are rightly highly regarded. We calculate and want to have everything under control. In the process, however, meaningfulness is often lost and frequently the relevance of a perfect demonstration of thought can no longer be found. Romanticism recognised this very clearly and located essential humanity in poetic thought. Novalis wrote:

When figures and numeric shapes,
No longer show us moons or apes;
When those who merely kiss and sing,
Trump scholars taught in everything;
When to free life the world retreats,
And in the world this free heart beats;
When then anew by light and shade,
True clarity will be displayed;
When we in fairy tales and verse,
See history from its first birth;

> Then at One secret word's delight,
> This whole wrong being will take flight.
> (Translation by Hadi K. Deeb)

Nonetheless, the Romantics were firmly rooted in life – Novalis was an engineer. He suffered from a division of the spheres of life, however, and sought a connection between world and spirit, between life and art. It almost seems as if relevance and precision are opposing qualities. In the precise work of analytical-scientific thinking, relevance often gets buried and must first be uncovered, whereas in the relevance approach of poetic-comprehensive thinking, the precision of derivation is often missing. They are complementary ways of thinking. This has to do with the fact that human life takes place on different levels: in addition to reality (Realität) – to which humans do not have direct access, but only a constructed and mediated one – humans must gain their actuality (Wirklichkeit) in each case by putting their mind in relationship to it. This is not an unquestionable state that one simply inhabits, but, once accessed, it allows for presence. For the step taken towards the world, *things show appreciation (die Dinge zeigen sich erkenntlich)*, to borrow Peter Handke's beautiful formulation.

Reality is complex; one kind of thinking alone won't get to grips with it – it always needs a diversity of perspectives. Poetic thinking is always paradoxical thinking, since the world, like art, can fortunately never be fully grasped. Much is accomplished by becoming fully a part of it in moments of presence and incorporating such states into one's consciousness of the world. In the field of consciousness, the only progress is through obstacles. Only by running up against the various pockets of resistance of the mind can it be broadened. Only in this way, like an echo sounder, can one plumb the deep sea of the mind.

Since we cannot have direct access to reality, our thinking is less about reality and more about our access to it. The approach to reality determines it. It is the world won by us – actuality. Poetic thinking opens and cultivates ways towards this actuality through dialogical thinking and language thinking. The categories of attitude or mood, atmosphere and presence discussed above are also part of it. In this way we expand our concept of reason and can become more just in relation to life and our world.

Poetic thinking thinks the transformation process of things in actuality and presence. It is therefore fundamental for a different worldview and self-image, in which people define themselves through the moment of the present: in other words, through being together and living together with the world instead of dominating it. Poetic thinking explodes any framework; it is that which cannot be classified. That is why it is an agent of change, and a dangerous and necessary one at that. That is also why it finds itself repeatedly destabilising functional conceptual thinking, which is why the latter wants to suppress it. But without the meaning-constituting power of poetic thinking, humanity would lose not only what is specific to it but also its chances of survival.

However, poetic thinking does not want to fight conceptual thinking at all. The latter is just as necessary; poetic thinking takes aim only at its claim to exclusivity. Just as poetic thinking alone could not last, so conceptual thinking alone would ultimately be meaningless. A final rational justification is impossible. Poetic thinking places itself in a tradition of thought that leads from idealism via Feuerbach, Nietzsche, the dialogists, Heidegger, Adorno and Derrida to contemporary aesthetics, which attempts to deal with this aporia of conceptual thinking.

Even if poetic thinking can only ever exist as a complement to conceptual thinking and to the I-It world, it is nonetheless an indispensable part of human life since it transcends human action and its rationality in an immanent transcendence. Without this transcendence, human beings would lack the superior meaning of life and the openness of possibilities; they would remain trapped and limited in the factual, and in the long run they would lose the flexibility and capacity for innovation necessary for survival. Poetic thinking is therefore about the role that the spiritual, cultural and historical play in the definition of humanity and of life, and thus about a resistance to the current dominance of biologically understood life sciences in the guiding concepts of the human and of society. Poetic thinking is, then, the necessary corrective and the necessary complement to the functional – each needs the other.

There is a complementarity of I-You world and I-It world, of sign and beyond the sign, of system and system subversion. Paradoxically, the system requires a space that breaks through the system. Poetic thinking shows limits to systemic thinking and so keeps it open, so that the system does not become encrusted.

A system is necessary for every community. Poetic thinking, in turn, is necessary so that the community is not subsumed by the functional with the result that it ultimately perishes, but instead it remains human and capable of survival. It does not want to "defeat" the system, it is rather the perpetually other of the system. The potentiality of poetic thinking penetrates the space of systemic thinking as a necessary corrective; it passes through this space, not over it. But it need not be in rivalry with the system; they are two different worlds that co-exist and both have their justification, complementing one another. A balance should, however, be maintained; as soon as one part usurps all the space, the world gets out of joint.

Poetic thinking is not exclusively concerned with translating the experience of the unspeakable into language after all, and thus with widening the boundaries of the human and keeping them open, but also – as we have seen in the reflections on language thinking – with the possibilities of having experiences in and with language that go beyond the existing in the first place, and of bringing these experiences into consciousness as elements that shape our view of the world. Poetic thinking seeks to co-develop forms of discourse that bridge the gap between experiences of transcendence and conceptual thought. It is an aesthetic and anthropological thinking.

A certain attitude is the precondition for giving the necessary attention to language, the in-between and the atmospheres. One must turn towards the world for it to be appreciative. Interpersonal experiences and attitudes shape our brain, thinking, feeling, being – the attitude of poetic thinking is constitutive of reality. It is not a formulaic solution, a doctrine that one can simply follow. But its thematisation does not remain without effect, because *discourse* (in Foucault's sense as the totality of the ways of thematising a thing) determines being.

In a number of insights that anticipate both these ideas and today's brain research, Ludwig Feuerbach stated that we indeed have the necessary senses for that which interests us, and that materialism has brought about a loss of faith and with it a loss of the ability to perceive the non-sensual world. Accordingly, it depends on what one cultivates; this has much to do with one's own choices. We must develop exercises, Sloterdijk would say, which make us what we want to be. We have to know what we want, what we gain from our choices, and what we lose. It's a constant decision-making process – every moment anew.

By integrating poetic thinking into our view of the world, we attribute to it a reality-shaping effect. By cultivating this attitude, we engage in a practice that helps shape our being. If we want a more human world, we need to give more space to what constitutes our specificity as human beings. And we have found that the human consists of a surplus of which we can only become aware in poetic thinking.

Poetic thinking promotes creativity and flexibility without losing the interpersonal dimension and thus also comprehensibility and social cohesion. It gives form to a personal experience of life that includes others, remaining open to the future. In this respect it offers at the same time security and an awareness of diversity and variability – exactly what our era needs. Poetic thinking is potentialism: just as the cosmos is infinite, so we humans have incalculable possibilities. The mysteriousness of our ever-amazing world and our own existence must be preserved for us to have a future. Let us think poetically, now, so that the future remains open, time and again: now.

Sources

In this book, I have deliberately refrained from giving precise references to sources. The aim is to make the book as readable as possible and appeal also to non-professional readers, for whom an extensive footnote apparatus would only be a hindrance. This of course does not mean that with these considerations I am not connected to many leading thinkers, to whom I refer and whose thoughts and formulations I pick up, adopt and develop. For those who are interested in more precise scholarly references and an extensive bibliography, I refer you to my book *Poetisches Denken und die Frage nach dem Menschen. Grundzüge einer poetologischen Anthropologie*, Karl Alber Verlag, Freiburg im Breisgau 2012 (series "Dia-Logik"), in which I have treated the topic more extensively and academically and on which I draw extensively in this current work. Here I would like to mention only a few essential sources.

As a non-scientist, in physics and neurobiology I rely primarily on the following:

Joachim BAUER, *Warum ich fühle, was du fühlst. Intuitive Kommunikation und das Geheimnis der Spiegelneurone*, München 2006.
Hans-Peter DÜRR, *Warum es ums Ganze geht. Neues Denken für eine Welt im Umbruch*, Frankfurt am Main 2011.
Gerald HÜTHER, *Bedienungsanleitung für ein menschliches Gehirn*, Göttingen 2011.
Michael TOMASELLO, *The Cultural Origins of Human Cognition*, Cambridge, Mass.–London 1999.

Sources 91

With regard to anthropological positions, I draw on:

Hannah ARENDT, *Vita activa oder Vom tätigen Leben*, München–Zürich 2007.
Gernot BÖHME, *Anthropologie in pragmatischer Hinsicht. Darmstädter Vorlesungen*, Frankfurt am Main 1985.
Hartmut und Gernot BÖHME, *Das Andere der Vernunft. Zur Entwicklung von Rationalitätsstrukturen am Beispiel Kants*, Frankfurt am Main 1985.
Arnold GEHLEN, *Der Mensch. Seine Natur und seine Stellung in der Welt*, Gesamtausgabe, Band 3.1, Frankfurt am Main 1993.
Max HORKHEIMER, Theodor W. ADORNO, *Dialektik der Aufklärung*, Frankfurt am Main 1969.
Wolfram HOGREBE, *The Real Unknown. Ein Rückblick auf die Moraldebatte der letzten Jahre*, Jenaer philosophische Vorträge und Studien, Erlangen–Jena 2002.
Dietmar KAMPER, Christoph WULF (Hg.), *Anthropologie nach dem Tode des Menschen. Vervollkommnung und Unverbesserlichkeit*, Frankfurt am Main 1994.
Dietmar KAMPER, Christoph WULF (Hg.), *Logik und Leidenschaft. Erträge Historischer Anthropologie*, Berlin 2002.
Immanuel KANT, *Anthropologie in pragmatischer Hinsicht*, Werkausgabe, Band 12, Frankfurt am Main 1995.
Ernst TUGENDHAT, *Anthropologie statt Metaphysik*, München 2007.

The section on body thinking and hominal technologies picks up thoughts from the following among other sources:

Günther ANDERS, *Die Antiquiertheit des Menschen*, Band 1: Über die Seele im Zeitalter der zweiten industriellen Revolution, München 1956.
Gernot BÖHME, *Leibsein als Aufgabe. Leibphilosophie in pragmatischer Hinsicht*, Zug 2003.
Helmuth PLESSNER, *Anthropologie der Sinne*, Gesammelte Schriften, Band 3, Frankfurt am Main 1980.
Helmuth PLESSNER, *Über einige Motive der Philosophischen Anthropologie*, Gesammelte Schriften, Band 8, Frankfurt am Main 1983.

Günter SEUBOLD, *Die Zukunft des Menschen. Philosophische Ausblicke*, Bonn 1999.
Günter SEUBOLD (Hg.), *Humantechnologie und Menschenbild. Mit einem Blick auf Heidegger*, Bonn 2006.
Günter SEUBOLD, *Der idealische Körper. Philosophische Reflexionen über die Machtergreifung der Körpertechnologien*, Bonn 2008.

The reflections on life forms and biopolitics are mainly inspired by:

Giorgio AGAMBEN, *Mittel ohne Zweck. Noten zur Politik*, Freiburg–Berlin, 2001.
Giorgio AGAMBEN, *Homo Sacer. Die souveräne Macht und das nackte Leben*, Frankfurt am Main 2002.
Giorgio AGAMBEN, *Das Offene. Der Mensch und das Tier*, Frankfurt am Main 2003.
Wolfgang ASHOLT, Ottmar ETTE, *Literaturwissenschaft als Lebenswissenschaft. Programm – Projekte – Perspektiven*, Tübingen 2010.
Michel FOUCAULT, *In Verteidigung der Gesellschaft. Vorlesungen am Collège de France (1975–1976)*, Frankfurt am Main 1999.
Michel FOUCAULT, *Geschichte der Gouvernementalität II. Die Geburt der Biopolitik. Vorlesung am Collège de France 1978–1979*, Frankfurt am Main 2004.
Michel FOUCAULT, *Histoire de la sexualité* (3 Bände), Paris 1976–1984.
Peter SLOTERDIJK, *Regeln für den Menschenpark. Ein Antwortschreiben zu Heideggers Brief über den Humanismus*, Frankfurt am Main 1999.
Peter SLOTERDIJK, *Die Verachtung der Massen. Versuch über Kulturkämpfe in der modernen Gesellschaft*, Frankfurt am Main 2000.
Peter SLOTERDIJK, Hans-Jürgen HEINRICHS, *Die Sonne und der Tod. Dialogische Untersuchungen*, Frankfurt am Main 2001.
Peter SLOTERDIJK, *Du mußt dein Leben ändern. Über Anthropotechnik*, Frankfurt am Main 2009.

The thoughts on atmosphere and mood were stimulated by:

Martin BASFELD, Thomas KRACHT, *Subjekt und Wahrnehmung. Beiträge zu einer Anthropologie der Sinneserfahrung*, Basel 2002.

Gernot BÖHME, *Atmosphäre. Essays zur neuen Ästhetik*, Frankfurt am Main 1995.
Gernot BÖHME, *Anmutungen. Über das Atmosphärische*, Ostfildern vor Stuttgart 1998.
Hans Ulrich GUMBRECHT, *Stimmungen lesen. Über eine verdeckte Wirklichkeit der Literatur*, München 2011.

The concept of immanent transcendence is borrowed from:

Ernst TUGENDHAT, *Anthropologie statt Metaphysik*, München 2007.

And the reflections on presence follow:

Hans Ulrich GUMBRECHT, *Diesseits der Hermeneutik. Die Produktion von Präsenz*, Frankfurt am Main 2004.

In terms of language thinking, I owe much to Jürgen Trabant and Henri Meschonnic, especially:

Émile BENVENISTE, *Problèmes de linguistique générales 1 und 2*, Paris 1966 und 1974.
Henri MESCHONNIC, *Critique du rythme. Anthropologie historique du langage*, Lagrasse 1982.
Henri MESCHONNIC, *Politique du rythme, politique du sujet*, Lagrasse 1995.
Henri MESCHONNIC, *Dans le bois de la langue*, Paris 2008.
Henri MESCHONNIC, *Pour sortir du postmoderne*, Paris 2009.
Jürgen TRABANT, *Apeliotes oder Der Sinn der Sprache. Wilhelm von Humboldts Sprach-Bild*, München 1986.
Jürgen TRABANT, *Artikulationen. Historische Anthropologie der Sprache*, Frankfurt am Main 1998.
Jürgen TRABANT, *Mithridates im Paradies. Kleine Geschichte des Sprachdenkens*, München 2003.
Jürgen TRABANT, *Was ist Sprache?*, München 2008.
Jürgen TRABANT, *Die Sprache*, München 2009.

and of course:

Wilhelm von HUMBOLDT, von A. Leitzmann et al., *Gesammelte Schriften*, hrsg., (17 Bände), Berlin 1903–1936.

My remarks on dialogics refer to:

Jean-Luc NANCY, *Être singulier pluriel*, Paris 1996.
Peter SLOTERDIJK, *Sphären 1. Blasen*, Frankfurt am Main 1998.

and are based on:

Martin BUBER, Werke in drei Bänden, München–Heidelberg 1962.
Ferdinand EBNER, *Fragmente Aufsätze Aphorismen. Zu einer Pneumatologie des Wortes*, Schriften, Band 1, München 1963.
Ludwig FEUERBACH, *Grundsätze der Philosophie der Zukunft, Kritische Ausgabe mit Einleitung und Anmerkungen von Gerhart Schmidt*, Frankfurt am Main 1967.
Franz ROSENZWEIG, *Der Stern der Erlösung*, Frankfurt am Main 1990.
Franz ROSENZWEIG, "Das Neue Denken", in: *Zweistromland – kleinere Schriften zur Religion und Philosophie*, Berlin–Wien 2001.

Index

acroamatic 58–59, 74
actuality (Wirklichkeit) 8–12, 75, 79, 86–87; actualise/actualisation 9, 42, 45, 75–76, 78
aesthetic 24, 42, 45–47, 50, 87–88
Agamben, Giorgio 33
analysis, analytical 7, 9–11, 13, 23, 28, 32, 35, 46, 49, 56, 63, 66–67, 69, 86; analytical language 82; analytical philosophy 56, 60, 79
Anders, Günther 28
anthropology 15, 20, 22, 61, 65, 77, 88; anthropology of language 51; philosophical anthropology 22; physical anthropology 45; poetological anthropology 3, 21; potentialist anthropology 36, 45, 78, 84; pragmatic anthropology 21
art, the arts, artist 5, 29, 30, 32, 35–36, 41–43, 46, 49–50, 64–67, 78, 81, 86
ascesis 5, 40
atmosphere 8, 41–44, 86, 88
attitude 6, 8, 11, 23, 35, 37, 41, 43, 48, 60–61, 64, 75–76, 78–79, 81, 83–84, 86, 88–89

Bacon, Francis 56
being, the 4, 6, 11, 15, 19–20, 23–24, 26, 35–36, 38, 41–42, 44–49, 52, 54, 57, 65, 66–67, 69, 72, 75–81, 83–84, 86, 88–89;
being human, human being 15, 20–21, 23, 25–27, 29, 31–32, 34–36, 42, 45, 48, 50–51, 55, 61, 65, 70–73, 76–78, 84–85, 87, 89; being-in-relationship 41; being-with 73
Benjamin, Walter 42
Benveniste, Émile 63
biology, biological, biologist 14–15, 18–20, 35, 85, 87; biologism 51
body 3, 14, 18, 21, 23–31, 35, 42–43, 49, 84; body machine 26; body politic 34; body technologies 23
Böhme, Gernot 43
Bohr, Niels 8
Broglie, Louis-Victor Pierre Raymond de 8
Buber, Martin 71, 74–78

Christianity, Christian 28–29, 53, 74
Cognition, cognitive 15, 23, 52–53, 55, 59, 61, 76
Cohen, Hermann 71
conceptual, conceptualisation 11, 13, 30, 48, 70, 76, 87–88
conscious, consciousness 3, 23, 48, 54, 70, 79, 82
consumption/consumerism 3–4, 24, 81, 85
continuous, the 62–63

cultivate, cultivation 4–6, 19, 21, 36–41, 43, 49, 62, 64, 67–68, 73, 75, 78, 82, 86, 88–89

Derrida, Jacques 76, 87
dialogical, dialogics 43, 59, 64, 71, 73–74, 77–79, 82–84; dialogical thinking 69–72, 77–78, 86

Ebner, Ferdinand 71
education 1, 4, 7, 27, 31, 34, 38–39, 62, 71, 82
Einstein, Albert 8
encounter 32, 46, 59, 61, 69, 72, 74, 76–78, 82, 84
Enlightenment 2–3, 11, 21, 23, 27, 62, 69, 73
esoteric, esotericism 3, 12, 42, 58

fact, factual, facticity 32–33, 36, 56, 87
Feuerbach, Ludwig 70, 87–88
Foucault, Michel 5, 32, 38, 88

Goethe, Johann Wolfgang von 11, 17, 53
Gumbrecht, Hans Ulrich 49–50

Hamann, Johann Georg 70
Heidegger, Martin 87
Heisenberg, Werner 8, 12
Herder, Johann Gottfried 58, 70
Hölderlin, Friedrich 77
holistic (see also wholeness) 8, 10, 12, 17, 24, 26, 33, 50, 63, 77
humanities 7, 29, 32, 36–37, 77
Humboldt, Wilhelm von 51–52, 59–62, 65–66, 70, 72, 77

in-between, the 75, 77–78, 81, 84, 88
I-It 75–79, 87
I-You 75–79, 81, 84, 87

Jacobi, Friedrich Heinrich 70, 74

Kant, Immanuel 2, 21–22, 58

language thinking 44, 51, 57, 61–64, 66–67, 69, 72, 74, 77–78, 81–83, 86, 88; thinking language 51, 57
Leibniz, Gottfried Wilhelm 57–58
Liebrucks, Bruno 72
life sciences 31–33, 87
literature 7, 30, 37–38, 41, 64–67, 72
Locke, John 56
Loyola, Ignatius of 38

material, materialism 2–4, 9–12, 15, 25–26, 60–61, 81
medicine 25–26, 28
Meschonnic, Henri 62, 64, 78
Mettrie, Julian Offray de la 26
modern 56, 73
modernity 35, 54, 75
mood 18, 41–42, 58, 86
mystical, mysticism 46–48, 79

Nancy, Jean-Luc 72
neurobiology 14–15, 19
neuroscience 14, 18–20
Nietzsche, Friedrich 2–3, 19, 27, 45, 56, 77, 87
Novalis 41, 85–86

paradox 13, 48, 67, 80, 86–87
physical, physics 7–10, 12, 15–16, 19–20, 23, 25–27, 34, 37–39, 42, 45, 70; quantum physics 9–10, 12
Planck, Max 8
Plato 52, 63–64
poetic, the, poetical 5–6, 12, 21–22, 32–33, 41, 47, 52, 60–62, 64–67, 77, 79, 81, 83, 86
poetic thinking 1, 4–6, 12–13, 19–23, 29–35, 41, 43, 47–48, 50–52, 60, 64, 66–69, 71, 73, 77–89
politics 1–4, 33–35, 37, 42; biopolitics 34–35, 84
potential, potentiality 10–11, 20–21, 27, 31, 36, 45, 49, 65, 78, 84–85, 88–89

presence 5–6, 43, 45, 47–50, 67, 72, 74, 76–78, 80, 83, 86–87

reality 8–10, 12, 21, 27, 43, 64, 74–75, 83, 86, 88–89
reason 21, 58, 73–74, 79, 83, 86; the greater reason 3, 5–6, 15; the other of reason 21; instrumentalised reason 31
relationality 11, 43, 75–76
resonance 18–19, 73
rhythm 62–63
Romanticism 41, 85–86
Rosenstock, Eugen 71
Rosenzweig, Franz 71–72, 74
Rutherford, Ernest 8

Saussure, Ferdinand de 62
Schiller, Friedrich 6, 24
Schopenhauer, Arthur 74
science, scientific 7, 9–12, 14–15, 18–19, 23, 29–33, 42–43, 56, 66–67, 73–74, 85–87; life sciences 31–33
sign thinking 61–67, 77, 81, 83, 87
silence 45, 47–48, 50
Sloterdijk, Peter 5, 38–39, 72–73, 88

spiritual 3–4, 8–11, 15, 26–27, 37–39, 44–45, 55, 82, 87
Stanislavski, Konstantin 63
subject-object division/separation 70, 75–76
subject-object thinking 81, 83
subject-subject relationship 76–77

technology 6–7, 13, 23, 25, 27, 29, 35–36, 39–40
totalitarianism 21, 35, 61, 64, 67, 84
Trabant, Jürgen 60, 80, 82
transcendence 31, 45, 71, 75, 77, 84, 87–88; immanent transcendence 45–45, 79, 87
transformation 2, 66, 69, 78, 87
truth 9, 47–48, 56–57, 59–61, 64, 74

Weizenbaum, Joseph 29
wholeness 19, 65, 77
Wilde, Oscar 24
Wittgenstein, Ludwig 52, 56, 79
worldview 6–8, 11, 23, 32–33, 58–59, 61, 87